By Death or Divorce...
it hurts to lose

By Death or Divorce...
it hurts to lose

Amy Ross Young

ACCENT BOOKS
Denver, Colorado

 MEMBER OF
EVANGELICAL CHRISTIAN
PUBLISHERS ASSOCIATION

Second Printing

Accent Publications
12100 W. Sixth Avenue
P.O. Box 15337
Denver, Colorado 80215

Library of Congress Catalog Card Number: 76-8737

ISBN 0-916406-32-6

Foreword

A human touch and warmth of love enriches this book, *By Death or Divorce . . . It hurts to lose.* If death or divorce has touched your home or someone close to you, this book will cause you to probe your heart and turn to the God of all grace. The author writes from a heart bent on glorifying Christ in all the ups and downs of her experiences. The reality of Romans 8:28 is seen throughout. She does not try to write with the authority of a marriage counselor but with a deep concern that her life, with its sorrows and joys, will be used of God to lift others to rejoice in the victory that God gives.

It was my privilege to be Amy Young's pastor for several years in Denver, and she has been a close friend to our home through the years.

Amy Ross Young is a strong Christian and when we realized the depth of her background and heard her tell of her joys and struggles and triumphs, we hoped she would put it down to help others experiencing like problems. Obviously, this could not be an easy task, but we are glad she has done so. See your own life in it and find renewed hope as she shows you hers.

Hubert Verrill
Pastor of the First Baptist Church of Tempe
Tempe, Arizona

Dedication

To my son Ronnie . . .

who made it all the way from fourth grade to

Dr. L. Ronald Ross,

Professor of Linguistics,

in spite of the mistakes I made and partly because

of the things we did right together.

But mainly, because he is his father's son.

Appreciation

My Sincere Thanks . . .

To the many friends who prayed for me as I reopened the hurt and tears of the past.

To my dear friends, Bob and Lyda Mosier, and Maxine and Ed Dannenberg, who also had to relive the heartaches of the past as this book was written.

To my brother and his family, and others, for letting me include their heartaches.

To my friend and editor, Violet T. Pearson, for her constant encouragement and expert editing.

And last of all, to my son for his love and understanding and for letting me know a little more what he, too, went through in the loss of our "special person."

Amy Ross Young

Contents

A Two-Time Loser

*M*y life is happy. You could classify me as a "well-adjusted single person." Often alone, but seldom lonely, my world includes a dear family, wonderful friends and a challenging career in a Christian business. Each day is so full and moves so fast that there are never quite enough hours or minutes in it. There is always a waiting list of projects I hope to fit into the future: organ lessons; a course in Swedish; a class in ceramics, or macrame; another book to write; a return trip to Europe to see all of the exciting sights I missed the first time.

The cheery little song, "Count Your Many Blessings, Name Them One by One," often dances through my mind. Many times I have to do it on the run, but count them I must. For my Heavenly Father loves me, cares for my every need, knows all about me—my good points and my bad—and best of all, He understands me!

With all of this going for me, I had to be out of my mind to even consider writing a book on the subjects of death and divorce. To write it would mean looking back—and yes, reliving the hurt and heartaches that were safely buried in the annals of the past. Old wounds would have to be opened and recorded for all to see. I wasn't sure I was willing to pay that price.

Sharing my innermost thoughts, dreams—and heartaches—has always been difficult for me. No more than two, or three, very close friends have ever been thus exposed. I find it much easier to share someone else's heartache and to help others with their problems. Perhaps this leaves me less vulnerable. Or, it may be due in part to the executive position I hold. I cannot afford the luxury of self-pity, nor days of depression.

I struggled with the question, "to write, or not to write?" The decision, however, I had to admit, was not mine to make. It seemed that at every turn, the Lord was whispering, "I helped you through these heartaches, now share your victories with others who hurt."

Here's what started me thinking about such a book. About two years ago, I read an article listing the ten most traumatic experiences in life. Number one was, "The loss of a mate by death." I discovered that I could close my eyes and recall every detail of that Saturday night. The life of one very dear husband and father was snuffed out in a tragic accident. So alive one minute—gone the next. I would have to agree—it was the most traumatic experience of my life.

It was a time of heartache, shock, fear, frustration, loneliness—and mistakes. It was also a time of learning, growing, acceptance, adjustment and eventually victory and peace.

"The loss of one's mate through divorce," was second on the list. Years later, I lost my second mate. The proof is tucked away in my file in the form of a legal document titled, "Decree of Divorce." A second experience with the same end result. One day I was half of a pair—the next I was alone. Only those who have been thrust into this position can know the inner turmoil and pain of the weeks and months that follow.

I know many people who are widowed—or divorced, but few who are two-time losers. Would this give me a rather unique vantage point from which to view the two top traumas life has to offer?

One day a friend asked, "Which *do* you think is worse, losing a mate by death, or divorce?" I had to admit that I wasn't sure. Either way—it hurts. The first heartache came when I was young—barely thirty—with a son to raise. The second fell when I was a mature adult with a son who was grown, married and on his own. Each experience had its own peculiar set of problems and heartaches. In many ways, however, the adjustments were similar. Perhaps I was better equipped to cope with the second, for having been through the first.

That article was only the beginning. In the months to come it seemed that other articles and books on one or the other subject kept crossing my desk. Many fine ones were being written, but none seemed to be saying what was in my heart. Some were making an effort to justify divorce, or to build a defense against the mistreatment handed out by the church and society in general. This was not my purpose.

I finally realized that if God wanted me to write this book, no one else would be able to say what I wanted to say. It would have to be me—no matter what the cost. Looking back, I have to admit it was the hardest writing I have ever attempted. More than once, sobs shook my body as I relived the heartache of the first two chapters. I walked the floor and agonized over chapter three. There were days when I wanted to run, but the Lord had me committed to that typewriter.

My sincere prayer is that God will take my past heartache—shared as much as possible—and use it to encourage and comfort the newly brokenhearted. And that this book will prove to be a down-to-earth, day-to-day, help for the many men and women who know that *By Death or Divorce—It hurts to lose.*

1

By Death . . .

"*Thou numberest my wanderings; put thou my tears into thy bottle. Are they not in thy book?*"

Psalms 56:8

*T*he newspaper headline read, "He's Made Last Round—DOG KEEPS VAIN VIGIL FOR FRIENDLY POSTMAN." Excerpts from that newspaper article tell the story.

The kids and the dogs were waiting as usual at the corner mailboxes yesterday morning, but their friend didn't show up.

The dogs couldn't know it, but the children could be told. Their friend was the postman, and he wouldn't be making his rounds in Northwest Denver any more. He was dead.

Bob Ross wasn't just an ordinary postman, according to the people who lived on his route. He was a personal friend of everyone—dogs, kids, housewives, old ladies . . . just about everyone.

When they saw in Sunday's Rocky Mountain News that Bob was killed in the crash of his motor-scooter with an auto, they could hardly believe it.

Tears came to the eyes of some of the people. "Just two weeks ago," one lady said, "he came around to see all of us who used to be on his route. He apologized for being moved."

The neighbors got together yesterday to figure out some way of showing their grief at the friendly postman's death.

"We plan to take up a collection for his little boy, Ronnie," said Mrs. Hildreth. "We think we'll try to get a bond for him. He's only 9 years old. It would mean something to him someday."

The youthful carrier—he was only 32—seemed to have a lot of fun out of life. After he bought the scooter, he would ride it to work, pick up his mail, and then park it at Lindy's Garage. Often the kids and dogs would meet him there.

He told his "customers" about the scooter which took him to his death. "I took Ronnie for a ride," he said one day. "It rained and we got soaked, but we sure had a lot of fun."

Bob took an active interest in the affairs of his "customers." He worried with Mrs. Hall when her baby was sick. When Mrs. Hildreth's monthly check arrived, he would knock on her door and hand her the envelope.

"Here's your paycheck," he would say.

At the home of Mrs. Miltick, he used to ring the bell and call her to the door, for she was sick and couldn't make useless trips to look for the mail. He'd watch boxes across the street, and if he saw letters at a box, he'd cross and pick them up, whether he had mail for the house or not.

"Bob Ross," say his friends, "was the kind of a guy who helped the small fry across the streets on their way to school."

"We'll miss him," his friends said yesterday.

I keep that newspaper article, along with other "memories," in a special box. I don't need it to remind me how special Bob was, nor how it hurt to lose him.

Neither will I ever forget the four months before he died. In November, we celebrated our tenth anniversary. We moved into our new home and enjoyed our first Thanksgiving in it. December rushed by with Ronnie's ninth birthday party—and Christmas.

We moved happily through January and into February. This short month brought us Valentine's Day, a day for sweethearts, and the next day—my birthday. Ronnie proudly shared with his daddy, and carefully kept, the secret of a surprise birthday party. Everything was so right with our world.

And then, ten days later, my world and Ronnie's came to a screeching halt. Our "special person" was dead. The memories of that night are forever etched in the secret places of my mind and heart.

Friends coming and going.
  Friends coming and staying.
    Neighbors looking in at the windows.
Looking out the window and seeing the smashed scooter.
    Fixing tomato soup for Ronnie.
      Running the water for his bath.
Taking Bob's billfold from the State Patrolman.
Telephone calls being made to family in distant places.
  And—in between, the telephone ringing.
    Tucking Ronnie in bed.
      Ronnie reaching for his teddy bear.
    Realizing he hadn't slept with it for years!
  Trying to get some rest. Friends sitting by my bed.
      Thinking to myself,

"It isn't real. It's a nightmare. When I wake up
everything will be all right."
But of course, it wasn't.

Morning brought reality, mercifully dulled by shock and an
overall feeling of numbness. I moved mechanically through the
next three days making funeral arrangements and handling
necessary business details. The Lord blessed me with dear and
faithful friends who helped through every painful decision.

"How cruel," I once thought, "for the family to have to move so
quickly in making arrangements." But, I have changed my mind.
This very responsibility forces you to dress, get out of the house,
to think and make decisions. It is something that has to be done,
and somehow you get through it.

At the graveside the finality of death deals a blow to your
stomach—and it hurts. I remember the evening of Bob's funeral.
Ronnie and I were staying with Bob and Lyda Mosier, dear friends
who had taken us home with them the morning after the accident.
Friends and family gathered in their livingroom after the funeral.
The abundance of food on the diningroom table was evidence of
the many friends who cared.

I sat listening to bits and pieces of the conversation going on
around me. I felt strangely detached from it all, as if all feeling, or
reaction, had been suspended. But, it didn't last.

"I can hardly wait for fishing season to open," one of Bob's
friends innocently remarked. That's all it took. Bob loved to fish!
The numbness dropped from me like a protective shell and the
pain in my chest lay naked and bare. Sobbing, I ran from the room.
Later in the evening, our pastor, Dr. Sam Bradford, sat by my bed
reading God's Word and praying with me. Through my tears, I
said, "It feels as if half of my heart has been wrenched from my
body." He gently replied, "It has."

I didn't fully understand what he meant at the time, but since
then I have been able to look back and see the beautiful truth in his
statement. In Genesis 2:18, God said, "It is not good that man

should be alone." Then He made Eve and brought her to Adam. This was the first wedding and it was God who performed the ceremony.

In Genesis 2:23 and 24, that first husband said, "This is now bone of my bones, and flesh of my flesh; she shall be called Woman, because she was taken out of Man. Therefore shall a man leave his father and his mother, and shall cleave unto his wife; and they shall be one flesh."

Before you became husband and wife, you functioned as two separate individuals. But when you were united in marriage, you became "one flesh." Spiritually, physically and socially you merged into *one* couple instead of *two* singles. The death of one partner reverses this process and the separation is painful. The one remaining is thrust into being, once again, an individual person—and that hurts!

The loss of your "special person" may be so recent that the healing process has not yet begun. You may be wondering if your heartache will ever let up. It will—in time. Well meaning friends often say, "Hang in there. Time heals all wounds." The natural question is, "But how *much* time?" I can only answer, "Longer for some than others—but time does help."

If you are a born-again Christian, you have one half of the battle won. Your Heavenly Father understands your heartache and keeps a record of your every tear. David wrote, in Psalm 56:8, ". . . put thou my tears into thy bottle. Are they not in thy book?" And the Lord Jesus Christ offers you peace and comfort. In John 14:27, Jesus said, "Peace I leave with you, my peace I give unto you; not as the world giveth, give I unto you. Let not your heart be troubled, neither let it be afraid."

Sometimes, however, the problem is in accepting what He offers. Even for Christians. Perhaps if I share with you the problem I had accepting Bob's death, some of the mistakes I made—and victories won, it will help you avoid the mistakes and realize the victory—sooner.

Even as a child, *every* problem that came my way was a

challenge. Problems were to be solved, repaired, organized away—or ignored. Seemingly impossible obstacles only took a little more work and a bit longer to remove. And then—Bob was killed. Death, I painfully discovered, was the most irreversible problem I had ever encountered. I struggled inwardly with utter frustration. "Self-sufficient Amy" had finally come face to face with something she couldn't change! Or fix! This absolutely immovable fact followed me like a long shadow. I couldn't get away from it—and I didn't want to accept it.

I tried to pray, but a gigantic "Why?" hung like a thick cloud between my Lord and me. At best I could only utter, "Lord, help me." I would open my Bible, but the tears of frustration blurred the words.

People who can, with real sincerity and peace in their hearts, accept the death of their spouse without question, have always left me a bit awe-struck. Age and spiritual maturity at the time must have something to do with it, as well as the makeup of the individual personality. The Lord had something to teach this young widow and Bob's death was to be lesson number one. For five months the inner battle raged.

Summer came and I flew to California to attend a Leadership Training Conference at the Forest Home Conference Grounds. There I met Dr. Henrietta Mears. Sensing my need, she invited me to her cabin one afternoon. With a few well-aimed questions she went right to the heart of my problem. Leaning over and shaking her finger at me, she said, "Amy, God loves you and He knows what's best for you. Now stop fighting against His will for your life so He can use you. Let's pray." And when she said it like that, there was only one thing to do—pray.

God used that godly woman to help me accept the healing balm of my Saviour's love and before the week was over I was able to say, "I know not the way, but well I know my Guide." Psalm 143:8 and 10 became my daily prayer: "Cause me to hear thy loving-kindness in the morning; for in thee do I trust. Cause me to know the way wherein I should walk; for I lift up my soul unto thee. Teach me to do thy will; for thou art my God. Thy Spirit is good;

lead me in the land of uprightness."

I can't honestly say that that week on the "mountain top" solved all of my problems, nor did it turn me into a mature, accepting Christian overnight. But the battle was over and I was ready to listen to God's Word.

I suppose almost everyone who has lost the one they love through death can look back and say, "If I had it to do over, I would . . ." My list is long and at the very top: *I would not struggle against God's will for my life.* In God's divine wisdom, however, there is a reason for giving us hindsight rather than foresight. Foresight, we could not handle! But, we can look back and learn from experience. As a result, I'm sure God expects us to emerge a more refined instrument in His hands.

What did I learn? I discovered that I am not all-sufficient and that the course of my life is best left in the hands of God.

Oh, I do forget occasionally and try to tackle things alone—and in my own strength. Then I have to be reminded that "I can do all things [only] through Christ, who strengtheneth me" (Philippians 4:13). One day, while talking with the Lord, I said, "Lord, whatever it is you are trying to teach me, help me to learn it—QUICK."

You may have a completely different personality, a unique set of problems and frustrations, but one thing we do have in common. We can both find the answers to our problems—and the lessons to be learned—in God's Word.

Even the Apostle Paul struggled for a time with something he didn't want to accept. He refers to it as a "thorn in the flesh." Three times he asked God to remove it—and each time God said, "Not so, Paul." Then Paul learned what it was that God was trying to teach him. It is recorded for our help in II Corinthians 12:9.

"And he said unto me, My grace is sufficient for thee; for my strength is made perfect in weakness. Most gladly, therefore, will I rather glory in my infirmities, that the power of Christ may rest upon me." Paul ended verse 10 with, ". . . for when I am weak, then am I strong."

Perhaps you are saying, "But I can't cope with this heartache, the problems I have to face." Oh, but you can when you realize that God's grace *is* sufficient. Let Him comfort and strengthen you through His Word. When you admit your own weakness, your inability to cope—then He will give you strength.

My most serious mistake was resisting God's will, and questioning His right to take Bob from me, but there were others. When that State Patrolman held out Bob's billfold the night he was killed, I felt my knees begin to buckle. The pastor was standing beside me. He slipped his strong arm around my shoulders and said, "Steady, girl. You must be brave—for Ronnie's sake."

"Can you identify this?" the patrolman quietly asked. My hand trembled as I reached for the billfold. I opened it—and nodded.

That sixty seconds started me on a pattern of behavior that is next on my list of "if I had it to do overs." I didn't realize it then, but the burden of being brave had just been placed on my shoulders.

The Burden
of Being Brave

"Cast thy burden upon the Lord, and he shall sustain thee; he shall never suffer the righteous to be moved."

Psalms 55:22

*T*he way you handle this tragedy will make a lasting impression on Ronnie," I heard someone say.

"You must be brave—for Ronnie's sake," the pastor had said.

Overnight, I became "Brave Amy" with a new reputation to build. Maybe I couldn't bring Bob back, but I *would* be so brave that Ronnie's and my world would be right again!

Assuming the role of both father and mother, I tried to pick up the broken pieces of our own private world and glue them back together—with self-produced courage. How hard I worked at being brave is revealed in a letter I received just five weeks after Bob's funeral. Here are three paragraphs from that letter:

"I think you should know that you are a wonderful testimony to us, your Christian friends. How often I have put myself in your place, and wondered if I, like you, could meet others with a smiling face—even though there is a broken heart."

And farther down the page, "It was truly a wonderful thing for you to have had us all to your home the other night—it was a *courageous* thing on your part."

The letter ended, "We really understand what is behind that smile you so *bravely* wear before us all." It was signed,

Maryanna and Joe Hart.

It was a beautiful letter in its entirety and it was a source of real encouragement to me. Looking back, however, it reminds me just how heavy the burden of being brave really was. In my own strength, I'm afraid I was equating bravery with wearing a smile.

Eight months later, after I had stopped resisting the Lord's will for my life, I received another letter. I would like to share it with you.

Dear Amy,

Sometimes a little note does a bit to help a person along, and somehow, the Lord has constrained us to pause and write this ill-framed letter to tell you that we have you upon our hearts, and that we by no means have forgotten that there still must be a tremendous burden upon your own soul. We tell you this not to reopen those wounds, but to assure you that the burden you carry is often remembered before the Throne of Grace.

As we mentioned before, your testimony and your braveness have meant more to us than you will ever know. Truly the Grace of our wonderful Lord and Saviour has been manifest in your heart. The marvelous way that Ronnie is developing is certainly a monument to your Christian strength and devotion.

In the hurry and confusion of our busy lives, we unashamedly omit the all important privilege of just taking time to be nice to one another, but will you accept these hastily written words as an expression of our Christian love and concern; and realize that we are your friends in the Lord? If there is ever anything we can do to help you in any way, please do not hesitate to make it known. That's what Christian friends are for.

We count it a privilege to know you, Amy. May God bless you and Ronnie.

The Philibosians
Isaiah 58:11

These letters and many others warmed my heart. I have used these two, written months apart, to try to show the difference between being brave in *my* strength—and walking bravely in the *Lord's* strength. The brave smile I wore was only on the surface. When I finally turned my heartache and frustration over to my Heavenly Father, He gave me inner peace. I was still lonely—and I still made mistakes—but now my ability to walk bravely into the future came from the all-sufficient, ever-present Christ.

If I had it to do over—I would let God take care of the "bravery department" right from the beginning. I don't believe Ronnie saw me cry after the night of Bob's funeral. Not only was I determined to be both father and mother, but somehow, some way, I would bring the laughter back to his eyes.

But while I was trying to hide my sorrow and loneliness from him, he was trying to do the same for me. And for a nine-year-old boy, the burden of being brave should have been lifted. I could have done it simply by sharing, at least a part, of my sorrow with him. Then, he would not have been ashamed to let me see his.

If I could turn the pages of time back and relive that first week, I would take Ronnie in my arms and say something like this: "We have just lost the most precious person in our world and it hurts! I'm thankful you weren't on the motor-scooter with Daddy, for then I would have lost you both. It may get rough at times, but we'll make it with the Lord's help." Then, I would hold him while we cried together.

Ronnie and I were not the only ones, however, who tried to hide our sorrow. Friends and family were also determined to be brave. I didn't even see Bob's mother, or sister, shed a tear, yet I know their hearts were broken. Everyone seemed bent on "holding up well."

It would have been far better for Ronnie and me to have shared the tears—the sorrow—of others. Perhaps we would not have been so alone in ours had we felt the need to reach out and help someone else. Comfort could have flowed both directions. The spotlight of grief should not have been so completely focused on us. Friends and family should have been drawn together in the circle of its light. Yes, our need *was* special—but it wasn't the only need.

I tried to share this with a friend at lunch recently. Maxine and her husband, Ed Dannenberg, were two of the friends who came to stay the night Bob was killed. As we talked, at lunch, I said, "I never saw either you or Ed shed a tear. Yet I know you must have cried for Bob."

Fresh tears came to her eyes. "Oh, we cried all right," she softly replied. "But, we didn't let you see us."

I sensed anew the love expressed by friends and family as they, too, bore the burden of being brave. But, I think we all made a mistake. Could it be that as Christians, we expect too much of each other—and of ourselves? Perhaps it is the result of not really understanding what God's Word has to say about death.

In I Thessalonians 4:13-18, Paul writes, "But I would not have you to be ignorant, brethren, concerning them who are asleep, that ye sorrow not, even as others who have no hope." I'm afraid we sometimes place a period after "sorrow not." But read on.

"For if we believe that Jesus died and rose again, even so them also who sleep in Jesus will God bring with him. For this we say unto you by the word of the Lord, that we who are alive and remain unto the coming of the Lord shall not precede them who are asleep. For the Lord himself shall descend from heaven with a shout, with the voice of the archangel, and with the trump of God; and the dead in Christ shall rise first; Then we who are alive and remain shall be caught up together with them in the clouds, to meet the Lord in the air; and so shall we ever be with the Lord. *Wherefore, comfort one another with these words."*

Our family recently faced another tragic death. My nephew, Bill Veidmark, was killed in a water-skiing accident in Phoenix. My brother Arvid, so much like me, also fought the battle of not being able to "fix it." Only he let it all out—immediately. For two nights and a day he struggled with rebellion, frustration and doubt. Lois, his dear wife, and their other children prayed, talked and loved him through it.

My niece, Cathy, said, "Oh, Auntie, it was so pitiful, but the second day it was just as if our Heavenly Father reached down and put His everlasting arms around Daddy, and the healing process began."

I arrived in Phoenix the evening before the funeral and was taken immediately to the chapel where Bill's body lay. Bill's younger brother, Pete, met me at the door and with his arm around me, led me down the center aisle. Near the front of the chapel Arvid and Lois were talking with a small group of friends. As soon as he saw me, my brother slipped away. He took me in his arms and we cried together. Then, he led me to the casket where Lois joined us. We shared some of the precious memories we will always have of Bill. Some of them brought a smile to our lips. Arvid excused himself as he noticed a friend of Bill's enter the chapel. He met her about half way up the aisle. She put her head on his shoulder and he comforted her as she, too, cried at the loss of Bill.

Weary from the long day, I slipped into one of the pews and just watched. The scene was so different. Friends continued to arrive, expressing their sorrow and giving—and receiving—comfort. I couldn't help thanking the Lord that His refining process was beginning to show. We were definitely more spiritually mature this time.

The next day the entire family, all twenty-five of us, gathered in the livingroom. It was almost time to leave for the church and Bill's funeral. Since it was the first, and probably the last, time we would all be together in one room, Bill's older brother Arvid, Jr., gave us the details of the accident. He then read some of Bill's favorite passages of Scripture. My brother and a pastor friend prayed. It was an experience I'll never forget. Truly a hallowed time with the Lord.

There are still those "rough days," for Bill's family. "It's so hard to let him go," his mother cried not long ago. But we know that Bill is with the Lord and that someday we will be, too. And we "comfort one another with these words."

Yes, Christians have every right to sorrow at the loss of a loved one—and to express it through tears. It is excellent therapy for both men and women according to an article by Dr. Lindsay R. Curtis in his column "For WOMEN only."

> Our culture trains boys early to believe that it is unmanly to cry, that to shed tears is to be a coward. In the words of Ashley Montague, we have produced "a trained incapacity in the American male to cry."
>
> Crying, however, is as normal an emotional response as laughing and is designed by nature to restore mental and physical equilibrium during periods of great stress.
>
> In times of crisis the male is supposedly a pillar of strength, standing courageous and firm while his "weaker half" wallows woefully in her tears.
>
> In reality, the man may not bear up nearly as well as the woman. By refusing to cry he turns his emotions inward and "weeps" instead through his skin in the form of boils, eczema and other dermatological eruptions.
>
> Without the therapeutic release of crying, his emotions also may affect the respiratory system, appearing as asthma, or they may focus upon the gastrointestinal tract as colitis.
>
> Other negative reactions in this connection may

include heart problems, hypertension or even a so-called "nervous breakdown."

I am not suggesting that failure to cry per se is the direct cause of all such problems or that it will help to produce them in any given case.

In the words of Montague, however, ". . . it is agreed by most authorities that crying is a beneficial means of relieving the person of tensions which seek expression in this particular manner. It is far better that the energies which seek release in such emotional expression find an outlet in weeping than that they should be pent up to seek adventitious expression through the body."

Nor am I implying that we should abandon all self-control in the matter of crying, indulging ourselves in sentimentality and self-pity. There is much to be said for stoicism in the face of adversity, but there are also times in our lives when tears—tears of compassion, tears of balm for suffering and bereavement—are the best medicine nature can prescribe.

One of the most eloquent passages in all literature is found in the New Testament and contains two simple words: "Jesus wept."

I have a friend who suffered seventeen years of agony and guilt, because he would not let himself cry in the presence of tragedy. He recently shared his heartbreaking story with me. When he was in his early twenties, he was driving his mother and father from one state to another. The car was old, the tires bald, and it was raining. Driving much too fast, he ignored his father's admonition to "slow down." The car skidded and went over a steep embankment.

He and his father escaped injury—but his mother was instantly killed. His grief was compounded by the feeling that he was responsible for her death. He went through the next week, with its family gatherings, and the funeral, without shedding a tear. Each time the doorbell rang, he forced himself to answer it and on the way to the door he would say to himself, "Don't you dare cry!"

That first week turned into months and the months into years—and still no tears. Seventeen years later, his suppressed grief and imbedded sense of guilt caught up with him. This outstanding man with tremendous abilities and talent had a "nervous breakdown." He finally came face to face with the burden he had carried for so long. The tears he now shed brought the release that should have been his seventeen years earlier.

With fresh tears in his eyes, he concluded his story by saying, "No matter who it is, man or woman, boy or girl, it is absolutely essential that they express their grief and cry it out at the time of their loss."

If you are bearing the burden of being brave and are refusing to find release in tears, may I reach out to you and say, "I am sorry your 'special person' is gone," and weep with you in your loss? Then, can I point you to the Saviour who loved you so much that He was willing to die in your place—to pay the penalty for your sin? And He still loves you so much that He offers you His peace and comfort. He understands your heartache—and cares that you hurt. Let Him reach down and comfort you with His perfect love.

In Psalms 55:22 we find this promise, "Cast thy burden upon the Lord, and he shall sustain thee . . ." And if that isn't enough, look at I Peter 5:7. "Casting all your care upon him; for he careth for you."

I found these promises to be true when I lost Bob and just as true when years later, I lost my second "special person"—by divorce.

3

By Divorce . . .

"He healeth the broken in heart, and bindeth up their wounds. He appointeth the number of the stars; he calleth them all by their names. Great is our Lord, and of great power; his understanding is infinite."

Psalms 147:3-5

*B*y death, or divorce, it hurts to lose. Twenty-two years and three days after Bob was killed, my second marriage was legally terminated. The end didn't come as suddenly as it had the first time. Few divorces, however, do come as a complete surprise. Nor, is it possible to put your finger on the exact day and hour when the problem was born. For me, it took this marriage eight long months to die. It was almost as if a "marriage doctor" had announced, "The disease is terminal. It could go at any time."

If you don't want the marriage to die, you pray right up to the very end that somehow—someway—things will work out. Even after the judge says, "Divorce granted," there is still hope. This is one way that losing your mate by divorce differs from death. My hope, however, was short-lived. The week the divorce was final, I received word that Ray had remarried. In that moment all hope died—and I knew it was over.

Ten years earlier, no one could have made me believe that this marriage would not last "until death do us part." Ray and I had been going together for almost three years when we decided to get married. Ronnie was attending the University of the Americas, in Mexico City, when I broke the news of my coming marriage to him. His answer to my letter is priceless and I still enjoy reading it today.

> Dear Mom,
>
> I received your letter about ten minutes before I left for Amecameca, and although for my conscious it was quite a surprise, my subconscious was more surprised not to have received it sooner. My first impulse was to throw myself on the floor and scream, "Good grief! My mother's getting married! I'm being deserted! She's trading me in on a husband!" But part of being mature, is not throwing ourselves on the floor at the first impulse, but waiting for the second. If we still consider it necessary, we may then throw ourselves on the floor and scream.
>
> As I am making an all-out effort to become mature, I restrained myself. Although you may not believe it, I really do enjoy seeing you have someone to go bowling with. I really think you are far too young and beautiful to settle down and grow old all alone, and if I stand on my tiptoes and peek over my own jealousy, I find that I really am glad that you have someone that isn't likely to run off to Mexico and leave you by yourself. The truth of the matter is, that if you hadn't had Ray to look after you, I wouldn't have come to Mexico.
>
> Even though this is all very serious, the whole thing kind of makes me chuckle. We do everything backwards. Not only do we doubledate, but *I* have to give *YOU MY* blessing to get married! At any rate you have it, and I'm glad you have a guy that'll spoil you the

way you have spoiled me (although at times I DO think he goes overboard—not really.)

I feel as if I should tell you that I'm getting married too, so I won't intrude, but the truth of the matter is that I really have no such plans. So you might have to put up with me for a little while longer.

Love,
Ronnie

It should have been a good marriage and a lasting one. At times it was good—and it did last for almost nine and a half years. And then one day it was over and I was once again facing the future alone. And yet, I was never really alone, for my Lord and Saviour walked ever so closely with me through every heartache and problem—and helped me through each stage of recovery.

Some of the problems faced after the loss of a mate are the same—whether by death or divorce. And some are the same for men and women. For example, how many times have you turned over in bed and, half awake, reached out to touch your "special person" only to find their side of the bed empty? That sickening feeling of loneliness hits and, wide-awake, you realize your mate is gone.

There are several ways you can react. You can bury your head in your pillow and cry. And sometimes that helps. You can lie awake for hours feeling sorry for yourself. That doesn't help. Or, you can talk to the Lord and tell Him just how you feel. Then, if you can't get back to sleep, reach for your Bible.

I have been amazed at how many times a verse, or portion of Scripture, which I have read many times will seemingly leap from the page to meet my specific need of the hour. Psalms 147:3-5 is one example. "He healeth the broken in heart, and bindeth up their wounds. He appointeth the number of the stars; he calleth them all by their names. Great is our Lord, and of great power; his understanding is infinite." Oh, does He care and understand when you hurt!

Heartache will have one of two effects upon your life. It will either draw you closer to God—or drive you away from Him. It will bring you into a sweeter fellowship with the Lord—or it will produce bitterness. It's all up to you. Life is too wonderful to waste feeling sorry for yourself and being down on the world. At least, not for very long.

Losing a mate by death, or divorce, is miserably sad and you have a right to indulge in a certain amount of self-pity. But don't remain in this state too long, for you have a job to do. Your goal is—recovery from a broken heart, a wounded ego; the rebuilding of a life; the rediscovery of your own personality; and last, but not least, learning to live with, and to like yourself!

After losing by death this should be the easiest. If you know that your mate loved you before death, you can have a good feeling about yourself. You feel loved. And, if you loved your mate in return, you do not have to wrestle with guilt or doubts about yourself. And even if your "special person" had a few flaws, they will soon be forgotten. Only the happiest memories of your life together will remain.

After divorce, it's a different scene. I'll review a few of the phases of recovery I went through before my flag of victory went up. You may be right in the middle of one of these stages. If you are, hang on and we'll try to pull you through.

"He doesn't love me any more!" Incredible! And I might add, a severe blow to my ego. This was the first reaction I had to cope with. I was *unloved*—and it hurt. Then one morning as I was reading in I John 4, I discovered in a new way, verses 10 and 11: "Herein is love, not that we loved God, but that he loved us, and sent his Son to be the propitiation for our sins. Beloved, if God so loved us, we ought also to love one another." I had read this many times, but I had never really *needed* it as I did that day. I wasn't unloved at all! God loved me more than any human being possibly could.

Having settled the problem of being unloved, the next emotional crisis reared its head. *Rejected!* Ray had said, "I want out." He was casting me out of his life. He didn't care what happened to me. I was being discarded. My wounded ego cried, "Ouch!" Even in less intimate relationships than marriage we don't like being rejected. It's a step beyond not being loved.

If you are trying to cope with your upset emotions after death—or divorce—in your own strength, please don't! God's Word is so full of His love, understanding and help. I found myself opening my Bible each morning with a real sense of anticipation—wondering which need He would meet for that day.

Here's how I got beyond the rejection phase. Ephesians 1:3-6 covers it all: "Blessed be the God and Father of our Lord Jesus Christ, who hath blessed us with all spiritual blessings in heavenly places in Christ, According as he hath *chosen* us in him before the foundation of the world, that we should be holy and without blame before him, in love. Having predestinated us unto the *adoption* of sons by Jesus Christ to himself, according to the good pleasure of his will, To the praise of the glory of his grace, through which he hath made us *accepted* in the Beloved." My Heavenly Father does not reject me! I am chosen, adopted and accepted by Him.

I jumped from rejection right into the middle of, "*Where did I fail?*" This one didn't weigh me down like "unloved," and "rejected." It just sort of chewed at me. Every divorced person would like to believe that the problem was one-sided. My loyal friends were quick to assure me that it was so. But every honest divorced person has to admit that it takes two to succeed—and two to fail.

Believe it or not, I couldn't find anything in God's Word that said I had not failed in some way, but I did find the assurance in Lamentations 3:22-23 that God *never* fails. "It is because of the Lord's mercies that we are not consumed, because his compassions fail not. They are new every morning; great is thy faithfulness." I just committed the whole failure problem to the Lord.

"*I'm not complete,*" was standing in line ready to take over where "failure" left off. There is something so nice about being part of a "Mr. and Mrs. Somebody." Have you ever noticed how comfortable and complete it sounds? Whether death, or divorce, turns it into "Mr. Only," or "Mrs. Only," it looks unfinished—incomplete.

In death the break is clean, finished—done. But in divorce it's not that way. Somewhere out there your ex-special person is walking around, living, breathing and probably not as unhappy as you are. You feel so cut loose.

Dr. Hubert Verrill, our former pastor, and his wife Evelyn were friends indeed. They went through most of these phases with me. I still marvel at their patience. One day I called them in Arizona and said, "You know that business about feeling incomplete? I discovered that I'm not at all!" Then I shared with them the Scripture I had read just that morning. Six simple words, which I had read dozens of times before, jumped right out of the chapter I was reading—and another problem bit the dust. Colossians 2:9-10a: "For in him dwelleth all the fullness of the Godhead bodily. And *ye are complete in him* . . ."

Are you beginning to believe that God's Word does have the answer to our every need?

There is another problem for the divorced or widowed person. It is a by-product of all the rest. *"I'm un-important"* is the label it wears. The most severe attack of this ailment comes to those without children, or to those whose children are grown and on their own. There is no one to care when, or even if, you come home in the evening. No one to care if you lose your appetite, how you look, or if the bed goes unmade all day.

This attitude is a downer that can make your life miserable. Every day is "blue Monday." It has to go! I was telling a friend this recently and she laughed and said, "I know—this is where you are going to use the 139th Psalm." She was so right. It just has to be my favorite portion of Scripture. Let me share the first ten verses with you.

"O Lord, thou hast searched me, and known me. Thou knowest my downsitting and mine uprising; thou understandest my thought afar off. Thou compassest my path and my lying down, and art acquainted with all my ways. For there is not a word in my tongue, but, lo, O Lord, thou knowest it altogether. Thou has beset me behind and before, and laid thine hand upon me. Such knowledge is too wonderful for me; it is high, I cannot attain unto it. Whither shall I go from thy Spirit? Or whither shall I flee from thy presence? If I ascend up into heaven, thou art there; if I make my bed in sheol, behold, thou art there. If I take the wings of the morning, and dwell in the uttermost parts of the sea, Even there shall thy hand lead me, and thy right hand shall hold me."

Read it again, and again, until it sinks in. Think about it. God knows everything about you. What you do, think or say—and all before it even happens. He is acquainted with you—completely! He goes before you and He follows from behind. You are surrounded by His love and care. And—He has laid His hand upon you. Wherever you are, He is there.

You *know* that God loves you, but do you realize that He also *likes* you? Just the way you are. Knowing everything about you, your failures, your doubts, fears and heartaches. He still likes you—and me.

Trying to prepare a young friend who was contemplating a divorce from his wife, I reviewed the stages of recovery he would have to face in the months ahead. Unloved, rejected, a failure, incomplete, unimportant, disgraced—and maybe a few of his own.

"I've felt all six in three days!" he miserably admitted.

For me, most of these phases took place from the time the divorce was filed until it was final—five months later. I admit that some of them slipped back occasionally, in the quiet of the night, or on a bleak and dreary day. But the closer I drew to the Lord, the farther apart the bad days were.

I did not contest the divorce, nor appear in court for the hearing. My lawyer represented me and reported to me later in the day that the divorce had been granted. Hearing it, however, did not make it real. Thus the big jolt was reserved until a few days later when I opened the envelope from my lawyer and held in my hands a piece of paper headed, "Divorce Decree."

DIVORCED! It rang in my ears. "In The District Court, Case No. 39302. It is Ordered, Adjudged and Decreed that a divorce be granted and the marriage between plaintiff and defendant is hereby dissolved." Now, it was real.

My thoughts began to race. Did this make me a second, or even third-class citizen? For over twenty years, an executive in a Christian business; seventeen years working with the youth in my church; Sunday School teacher all the way from Juniors up to Senior citizens. From first-class citizen—to third—in one easy divorce?

I don't like being divorced. I have no intention of trying to justify it, defend it, or recommend it. It should be reserved for the birds! In applying for a loan to purchase a condominium recently, the loan officer at the bank asked, "Widowed, or divorced?" I almost said, "Both." But I dutifully replied, "Divorced." I don't even like the sound of the word.

It is, however, here to stay. It is happening everyday, to Christians and non-Christians; to young couples and couples who have been married for years. Sometimes it is a Mom and Dad, son or daughter, aunt and uncle, brother or sister, nephew or niece, cousin or friend. The National Center for Health Statistics has recently announced that "The number of divorces in America in one year passed the one-million mark for the first time in history last year."

Dr. Paul Glick, senior demographer with the U.S. Census Bureau reported, "Based on 1971 data, 29 per cent of American marriages end in divorce, but we think that will increase to about 33 per cent, using new figures." Few people have not been touched by divorce. That doesn't make it good. But, perhaps it does make society more sympathetic to the heartache and problems faced by those who are the victims of divorce.

After losing by divorce, or death, the battle of emotional problems has to be fought and conquered. Emotional problems, however, are like a great backdrop against which we are required to perform the routine activities of everyday life. Each new day, week, or month brings its own down-to-earth, practical adjustments. They can be challenging, frustrating and sometimes even funny. And then, there are those that come straight from the panic department.

4

Don't Panic!

"And he was in the stern of the boat, asleep on a pillow; and they awake him, and say unto him, Master, carest thou not that we perish? And he arose, and rebuked the wind, and said unto the sea, Peace, be still. And the wind ceased, and there was a great calm. And he said unto them, Why are ye so fearful? How is it that ye have no faith?"

Mark 4:38-40

*T*he papers will be served on the 14th," my husband announced. "That will give you two weeks to find a place to live and move out."

Our beautiful home had been sold the week before, just three days after we had put it on the market. It had been over twenty-one years since I had lived in a rented house, or apartment. It was frightening to even think of looking for one now. Ray had prepared a "his" and "hers" list dividing our eight rooms of furniture—big furniture. As I reviewed "hers" some of the items seemed to get larger by the minute.

King-sized bedroom set
Four-foot-wide hutch
Five-foot-long buffet

> Seven-foot harvest table
> Eight-foot couch
> Tea cart

And—an orthopedic contour chair. *It* took up a third of any room it landed in.

I panicked!

Grabbing the evening paper, I circled the apartments that sounded promising—or even possible; jumped in the car and started dashing from one address to another. I quickly evaluated each potential "home" by stepping off the bedroom to see if the king-sized bed would fit, and tried mentally to squeeze that dining-room set into each tiny breakfast nook! If the bedroom was large enough, there was no place for the contour chair. If I found one with a diningroom, the bedroom was barely ten by ten. I just couldn't get it all together.

Dashing back to the car, after inspecting apartment number five, I started to laugh, partly from fatigue, but mostly because in the midst of this panic-riden evening something was funny. Here I was, running around like a chicken with a chopped-off head, trying to find a place to live—in my own strength! I thought I had learned that lesson long ago.

Burying my head in my arms on the steering wheel, I began to pray, "Lord forgive me. I know that You have just the right place for me. I'm going home and get some sleep. Please show me the apartment you have prepared for this emergency." With peace in my heart, I turned the car around and drove home.

Before I left my room the next morning, I once again opened my Bible to the 143rd Psalm. David always seems to say what is on my heart better than I can, so I made verses 7 and 8 my prayer for the day.

"Hear me speedily, O Lord; my spirit faileth. Hide not thy face from me, lest I be like unto them that go down into the pit. Cause me to hear thy lovingkindness in the morning; for in thee do I trust. Cause me to know the way wherein I should walk; for I lift up my soul unto thee."

A speedy answer was what I needed. There was only one more weekend before "moving day." I remembered hearing of a computerized rental service. I made one telephone call, telling the person on the other end of the line everything I needed in an apartment. Within a few minutes, she called back.

"We have just the place for you."

I called the number she gave me and in thirty minutes I was standing right in the middle of God's perfect provision. To my delight, it turned out to be a lovely ranch-style duplex. Now, why hadn't I thought of that? Bright red petunias lined the curved sidewalk leading to the front door. Inside, carpets, drapes and appliances were just the right color. And—there was even enough room for that contour chair. Not only did my Heavenly Father roll out a red carpet of petunias, He added more than I dared hope for: a garage, washer and dryer, a covered patio, and an outdoor fireplace.

What a tragedy it would have been if I had decided on an apartment the evening before. In my state of panic I would have completely missed the blessing of God's leading in my hour of need. Your problem may not be finding a new place to move into—almost overnight. It may be whether to sell your home, or to keep it. In either case, don't panic. Instead, ask the Lord to help you "know the way wherein [you] should walk."

A friend who is in the insurance business tells me there is one question he can count on when he calls in the home after the death of a husband or wife: "What will I *do?*"

"You will go on living," is his reply. He then explains that few decisions must be made immediately. "The important thing," he advises, "is not to panic. Wait a year, if possible, before making any major decisions or changes."

Whether you have been left alone as a result of death, or divorce, is relatively unimportant. Any day can deliver up a situation which rightly belongs in the panic department. Housing is just one of them. Others may not be quite so important, or serious.

The summer after Bob was killed, I had to make a decision that was almost as frightening as looking for that apartment. In retrospect, however, I have to laugh at the memory. Walking through the diningroom one day, I glanced out the window to see Ronnie walking very slowly and carefully up the walk. He was carrying something in his arms. I reached the front door at about the same time he did.

"Mom, look what I've got," he said with a note of wonderment in his voice.

He held out a soft black and white ball of fur for me to see. It was the most adorable puppy I had ever been that close to.

"Skip's dad says I can have her, if you say it's O.K."

"Oh, no!" I thought to myself. Then, panic set in. I had never had a dog in my life—only a little black kitten that grew into a big black cat that broke my heart when it disappeared. Neither Ronnie nor I knew anything about raising—or house-breaking—a puppy.

I began my defense.

"Honey, you will soon be going back to school and I'll be away at work all day. It wouldn't be fair to the puppy to be left alone all that time."

Somewhere this nine-year-old boy had learned that "All is fair in love and war." And I could see that he had already fallen in love with that wiggly ball of fur.

"Daddy *said* I could have a dog when we got our own house. *He promised.*"

Case dismissed. I wanted to say, "Then, why isn't he here to tell us what to do with her?" Instead, I said the only thing I could in light of the evidence.

"O.K., honey, you can have her—but you will have to take care of her—feeding, messes and all."

"I'm going to call her Tippy." The little rascal knew all along he was going to win.

Tippy soon became one of the family and she and Ronnie were inseparable. A lonely little boy had a friend. She seemed to understand that we knew nothing about puppies and literally house-broke herself. Friends marveled at our expertise, but we laughed and said it was just beginners' luck. I like to think, however, that it was because God cares about nine-year-old boys, puppies and a mother who was the victim of a juvenile con game.

No matter how slight, or serious, our problem is, it can be handled best without panic. Reading in the Gospel of Mark one day, I discovered a beautiful parallel between the disciples of Jesus and widowed and divorced people. Jesus had been teaching the multitude beside the sea. When evening came, He instructed His disciples to take the boat to the other side. Here is the account of their "stormy trip" as recorded in Mark 4:37-40.

"And there arose a great storm of wind, and the waves beat into the boat, so that it was now full. And he was in the stern of the boat, asleep on a pillow; and they awake him, and say unto him, Master, carest thou not that we perish?

"And he arose, and rebuked the wind, and said unto the sea, Peace, be still. And the wind ceased, and there was a great calm.

"And he said unto them, Why are ye so fearful? How is it that ye have no faith?"

It is so easy when the storms of life engulf you with loneliness and doubt, to wonder if the Lord is even aware that you hurt. Perhaps you cry out, much as the disciples did, "Don't You even care that I'm lonely and afraid?" And even as you turn to Him with such little faith, He replies, "Yes, I care." Then, He will whisper, "Peace, be still," to the winds that toss you to and fro. He is there in your struggle to find yourself, and to cope with each new problem.

Not only does the Lord know when we are about to panic because of some unusual circumstance, He also understands. He understands because of that day in the boat with His disciples. He knows the weakness of our humanity and stands ready to meet our every need.

To prove my point, I'll share with you one of my daily dreads. Silly though it was—the Lord understood. Living in the same town with your ex-spouse almost guarantees that sooner or later you are going to run into each other. I even rehearsed in my mind over and over what I would say should that moment ever arrive. "Hello, Ray. How are you?" Or, "Hi! Nice to see you again." Oh, I was going to be so casual.

Then, one day Maxine and I were hurrying through a department store in a nearby shopping center on our lunch hour. My hair was windblown and my face had red blotches on it. A hair spray allergy, my doctor had decided. I was definitely not at my best. All of a sudden, I caught a glimpse of a familiar figure about fifty feet away. I panicked! Grabbing Maxine's arm, I took a hasty detour into the cosmetic department. The moment I had been dreading had almost happened.

Realizing that I could not go through the rest of my life trying to avoid an encounter with Ray, I took it to the Lord. I prayed, "Father, please help me to relax in this matter. But, Lord, if I ever do run into him face to face please let it be after I have been to the beauty shop and not before."

Call it pride, or wounded ego. Ray had seen me at my best and also at my worst, so why should it matter? I don't know—it just did.

Several months later, my dear friend and editor, Violet T. Pearson, and I were having dinner one Sunday noon at a lovely restaurant across town. Vi has been alone for many years and knows and understands me like an open book. As the hostess led us to our table, I saw Ray, his new wife and his mother eating at a table near the window. I almost panicked when the hostess seated us not more than three feet from them. Vi didn't see them and I couldn't tell her for fear they would hear. One part of me read the menu and another part prayed, "Lord keep me calm. Give me poise."

As we waited for our salads to arrive, Vi chatted away completely at ease. I'm afraid I wasn't listening as closely as I should. I wanted to laugh. The Lord was actually humoring me. I was wearing a beautiful new soft blue knit dress and white sandals with just a touch of gold trim. And—my beauty operator had done herself proud the day before.

"Thank you, Lord, for understanding."

From just behind me, I heard the waiter say, "Thank you, sir, and have a nice day." The trio at the next table was preparing to leave. Ray's wife went quickly by. As Ray and his mother reached our table, I calmly looked up and said "Hi, Ray—Hello, Mom." His mother and I had been very close and I loved her very much. She stopped, took both of my hands in hers and we talked for just a brief moment and then they moved on.

"My, but you're the cool one," Vi said with amazement.

Smiling, I replied, "I had help."

From that day on, it has not mattered whether I run into him, or not. I don't think I would even care if I were on my way to the beauty shop. The Lord has healed my wounded ego.

You may have altogether different panic points from the ones I have shared. I can almost, however, guarantee that someday you will be able to look back and laugh at yourself. It is part of your recovery and it feels good.

But for now, remember that no matter how stormy your life seems, nor how prone you are to panic, the Lord understands and is just waiting to say "Peace, be still."

5

Wrestling With Responsibility

"Train up a child in the way he should go and, when he is old, he will not depart from it."

Proverbs 22:6

Who's gonna take me to Cub Scouts?" a solemn nine-year-old asked.

"I am, of course!" This was my first attempt at stepping into Bob's shoes.

The next evening, with a heavy heart, butterflies in my stomach and that "brave" smile on my face, I walked into the basement activity room of a neighborhood church with my son—who also had a heavy heart, butterflies in his stomach and a not-so-brave smile on his face. I doubt if he will ever let me know just what went on in his young head that night.

The room was filling up with loud and lively youngsters—all of the male gender. They were accompanied by the usual assortment of equally male dads. They treated me with sympathetic understanding, although they weren't quite certain how to react to a female "father" in their midst. But then I wasn't sure how to cope with a room full of the other kind, either.

We all managed to get through the evening, but on the way home Ronnie said, "Mom, you don't have to go every week. Maybe I can go with Skip and his dad." It sounded like a brilliant solution and I hastily agreed. I'm sure the Cub Scouts and their dads were relieved to discover my early retirement from their organization!

I cried myself to sleep that night, feeling I had failed in my responsibility and aching with loneliness for that nine-year-old boy's father. I should have realized right then that being a good mother to Ronnie was more important than trying to fill both roles. But, I was determined.

Wrestling with his daddy, was one of Ronnie's favorite sports. You guessed it. I tried to pick up where Bob left off. Fortunately, our matches were few and far between. When he was nine years of age I had little trouble "pinning" Ronnie to the floor, but one day when he was nearly eleven—he pinned me. At that moment my wrestling days were over. A son who was able to get the best of his Mom in a wrestling match could be difficult to discipline in more serious moments.

Children of divorced parents, or those who have lost one parent through death, do have special needs. And this is just another way of saying that *you* have special responsibilities.

Emotionally your child needs reassurance. When Ronnie asked who would be taking him to Cub Scouts, he was telling me that he missed his daddy. Even though my going wasn't the permanent answer, it did prove on that first night that he was not all alone. I don't think any friend, or neighbor, could have filled that need—on that particular night.

Emotionally your child needs physical contact. Ronnie and his daddy were very close. He often rode on the motor-scooter with his arms around his daddy's waist. When he was little he rode on Bob's back, or his shoulders. Later they boxed, wrestled, or just plain rough-housed it up. When he wanted me to wrestle with him, again he was lonely for the contact he had had with Bob. He may have been testing me as well, to see if I were really adequate for this job as single parent.

Emotionally your child needs the security of your love. Expressing it is your responsibility—in your own way. Ronnie had been raised in an atmosphere of love. He knew that Bob and I loved each other and he was secure in our love for him. After Bob was gone, however, I realized that he had been the one to set the pace for our openly expressing that love. Ronnie and I would now have to find our own way. We were much alike and it was difficult for us to say what was on our hearts. Yet, I knew we had to express it. I made it a nightly practice when I went to his room to tell him goodnight, to leave with something like this: "Hey, fellow, do you know that I love you very much?" He would usually answer, "I love you, too." Even today, words don't come easy, but we both know!

Your child also needs the emotional security of discipline. Many wayward young people have expressed the belief that if their parents had loved them, they would have disciplined them. Discipline, however, should always be for the good of the child and not for your own. Don't take your frustrations, anger, and loneliness out on your child.

Bob took the major responsibility for the discipline of our son. Some thought him a bit too strict, but he really was fair—and consistent. If he promised a spanking for an act of disobedience—he delivered. If he said, "No," to something—he meant it. Ronnie was never uncertain about the rules. This foundational training made it much easier for me when I had to pick up the reins of discipline.

I'll never forget the last spanking I ever gave Ronnie. And neither will he! He was in the ninth grade and almost fifteen years old. Lyda Mosier, who then lived just behind us on the next street, phoned me at the publishing house one afternoon.

"I thought you would want to know," she said, trying to be calm, "that Ronnie just went through our yard on his bike with a lead pipe in his hand. He is on his way to a gang fight between the seniors of Wheat Ridge and Arvada High Schools."

I had visions of him bashing some boy's brains out—or getting his own in the way of someone else's lead pipe. Bob Mosier, my boss, rushed me to the scene of the impending fight. Ronnie and a couple of his friends were safely observing from a block away as the older boys gathered. As we pulled up alongside his bike, I rolled the window down and ever so calmly said, "I'll give you just five minutes to get home." He made it in less.

We faced each other in the livingroom and he listened as I explained why I could not allow him to get involved in a gang fight. I concluded our "discussion" by announcing that I would have to spank him—to help him remember. I have to laugh when I run that scene through replay.

I went to the kitchen to get the strap used for such occasions. It was the kind mailmen use to fasten bundles of mail together. Bob had brought it home when Ronnie was about three years old. When I returned, this young man, now taller than his Mom, calmly reached into his left hip pocket and removed his billfold and into his right pocket to take out his comb. He placed them on the nearest end table, and with an air of tolerance, put his hands on his knees and bent over to receive the last whipping of his life.

It was almost as if he were saying, "This is ridiculous, but if you feel you have to do it—I'll cooperate." I have often marveled at the patience and the wisdom of my son and wondered just who did the raising.

I don't remember just when it happened in our days and months of recovery, but it did help when I stopped trying to be both a father and a mother and accepted the singular responsibility of raising a son. We both relaxed and our relationship settled into one of respect, love—and friendship.

There are other responsibilities that weigh heavily upon the single parent. Most of them fall into one of these categories: mental, physical, social, or spiritual. The comforting part is that with these you have a lot of outside help. The schools, your church, the community and the medical profession all stand ready to do their part, but don't expect them to do yours.

A recently bereaved friend once asked, "Where did you find the courage and wisdom to raise your son alone?" I replied, "I prayed a lot." I prayed for wisdom every day; I prayed that God would allow me to live to raise him to manhood; and that he would be a mature Christian when he got there. I was too frightened of the responsibility to have tried it without the Lord's help. More than once I reminded God of His promise in Proverbs 22:6.

"Train up a child in the way he should go and when he is old, he will not depart from it."

Responsibilities wear many different faces. Rearing children is only one. The mechanics of running a home is another that must be wrestled with. If you were married to a "handy man" you will probably find blown fuses, leaky faucets, stopped-up toilets and broken windows to be near disasters.

If, you as a man, never shared the household chores with your wife, a pile of dirty clothes, a greasy stove and a cluttered house can give you an ulcer—and send you straight to the computerized mating service. Don't despair and don't rush into marriage. Give yourself time to learn—and to heal. You'll be a happier person for it.

Start by making a list of emergency and service telephone numbers. Keep it by the telephone at all times. Here are a few suggestions: Police; Fire Station; Family Doctor; Hospital Emergency Room; Ambulance; Plumber; Glass Company; Electrician. I carry the business card in my billfold of a man who lists his profession as "HANDY MAN."

Next, determine to learn how to perform your new tasks. You can get a liberal education from family members, friends, neighbors—and even books and magazine articles. One such book is, *H.E.L.P. Home Emergency Ladies' Pal.* Here are the subjects covered: Emergency Home Supplies; Electrical; Gas; Plumbing; Carpentry; Emergency Medical Aid; Going Away?; and finally, A Woman's Guide to Survival. It's even a good book for a man to have around the house. Another source of information is the Owner's Manual that comes with most appliances. If you don't already know how, you can learn to operate the washer, dryer, sweeper, stove, can opener and almost any other gadget you happen to have.

How you wrestle with these new responsibilities is up to you. Either you will come out on top—or they will. I accepted some of the manly jobs as a challenge. We had a frame house and just about every three years it needed painting. A small bungalow in reality, it took on gigantic proportions the first time I tried to scrape, sand and apply those gallons of paint to its four sides. As a result, I am not afraid to tackle *almost* any painting job.

Our new power lawn mower was something else. It decided that *I* was a challenge! In utter despair, I have stood beside it and bawled because that piece of machinery would not start. Let a man approach it and it would take off on the first pull of the rope.

Is it easier for the father, or the mother, to be that one parent? I'm sure it depends much on the individual and the circumstances. If the mother has the ability to financially support the family, the rest she can probably cope with. She is already an experienced cook, cleaning lady, chauffeur, nurse and cheer leader. And, perhaps she can better understand the emotional needs of the children.

While a father may find it easier to provide for the financial needs of his family, he may not be as adept in the other areas. Some men, however, quickly learn to handle homemaking responsibilities. Others look for the solution in remarriage.

Divorced parents face a somewhat different picture. One parent usually has custody of the children, but both parents do still exist. The "outside parent" continues to have contact with, and the opportunity to influence, the children. And emergencies almost always rally the attention of both parents.

Managing a home and a family is always easier and more fun when there are two parents. We have already agreed that being a "one parent" person hurts. And sometimes this hurt makes the responsibility overpowering. But God only expects us to live one day at a time. In Matthew 6:34 the Lord ends his discourse on anxiety and worry. "Be therefore, not anxious about tomorrow; for tomorrow will be anxious for the things of itself. Sufficient unto the day is its own evil." The word evil denotes trouble or misfortune. You have enough responsibility, concern and heartache to wrestle with today.

Will Rogers once said, "Don't let yesterday use up too much of today." Whether your problem is living in your yesterdays, or worring about your tomorrows, Psalms 118:24 has the answer. "*This* is the day which the Lord hath made; we will rejoice and be glad in *it.*" I know you still hurt and can't blot out the past overnight, nor can you ignore the tomorrows completely, but taking life one day at a time is a much easier package to handle. Why not ask the Lord to make you the best Mom, or Dad, or single person needed to cope with those responsibilities before you—just for today?

6

Fighting Fears

"When thou liest down, thou shalt not be afraid; yea, thou shalt lie down, and thy sleep shall be sweet."

Proverbs 3:24

*T*ippy barked—and Ronnie and I froze.

It was the first night that we were alone in our home. Bob and Lyda Mosier and their four year old daughter, Janelle, had been staying with us since Bob's death waiting for the home they were building, on the street just behind us, to be finished. They had moved in that day. And, our little house was suddenly very quiet.

We could always tell the difference between the bark Tippy reserved for another dog and the one she used to warn of an approaching human. Tonight it was her "people" bark. We slipped into the darkened kitchen and peeked out the window. A man from across the street had just cut through our yard on his way home. Ronnie put his arms around Tippy's neck and proudly said, "Good dog."

Later that night, lying in bed with my eyes wide open and my body as stiff as a board, I realized that except for my nine-year-old son, I was alone—and it was dark!

Why is it that the house-settling noises of the night seem so normal when your "special person" is beside you? And then, take on such an ominous meaning when you are alone? Sleep was slow in coming that night. As I tossed and turned, my loneliness took on a new dimension—fear.

The next day I tried to rationalize the problem. If I were to take work home at night and stay up very late, then perhaps I would be so tired that I could fall asleep the minute my head hit the pillow. I gave it a try. After Ronnie was in bed I would start typing. More than once my head would drop to my arms on the typewriter as I fought to stay awake. Falling into bed—I slept.

How long I could have kept this up, only the Lord knows. But one day, He seemed to say, "My child, you've had it!" A concerned friend handed me a note. All it said was, "Read Psalm 127:2 and Proverbs 3:34." Curious, I looked them up.

"It is vain for you to rise up early, to sit up late, to eat the bread of sorrows; for so he giveth his beloved sleep." In Proverbs, I found, "When thou liest down, thou shalt not be afraid; yea, thou shalt lie down, and thy sleep shall be sweet." With these promises I began the fight to conquer my fear of the dark.

Though some men may find themselves uncomfortably alone in the night, this fear is probably more common among the gals. My fear of the dark dated back to childhood and I was concerned that I might convey it to Ronnie. With Tippy sleeping by his bed each night, however, it seemed he was afraid of nothing.

I recently learned how wrong I was. While I was trying to hide my fears from him—he had a batch of his own to face. I'm not sure it would have been wise for me to have shared mine with him, but I certainly should have been more aware of his. I was mailing the rough draft of each chapter of this book to "Dr. L. Ronald Ross" to see if he minded having "Ronnie, the boy" such a vital part of the early chapters. After reading the above in this chapter, he wrote telling me for the first time how he felt as a boy. Here is part of that letter:

I feel you missed my true feelings a bit, which could be important when there are children involved. You assumed that when I went to bed at night with Tippy that I had no fears. I remember vividly the tremendous burden of being the only man in the house at nine years of age. I must have asked myself a thousand times what in the world I would do if I had to defend the fort against an intruder. I was also plagued by the fear that something would happen to you, and many times suppressed the desire to ask you to be extra careful when you crossed streets during the day!

I wish that nine-year-old boy had asked me to be careful just one time. Then perhaps I would have sensed the fear he was facing. Perhaps you can learn from our mistakes and be more sensitive to the fears of your children.

It was during this time that I first discovered the 139th Pslam. The impact of the first ten verses was saved until after the divorce when I would need them more, but verses 11 and 12 gave me exactly what I needed for that day. I wish now I had read and discussed them with Ronnie.

"If I say, Surely the darkness shall cover me; even the night shall be light about me. Yea, the darkness hideth not from thee, but the night shineth as the day; the darkness and the light are both alike to thee."

To my Heavenly Father who watches over me there is no night. No shadowy figures, or creaky noises to worry about. He sees through the night as if it were day! I was beginning to understand that I was in very good hands. With that I committed my fear of the dark to the Lord. Oh, there have been certain experiences that were momentarily frightening, but I was done with that always-there kind of fear.

Psalms 139: 17 and 18 were an extra bonus. "How precious also are thy thoughts unto me, O God! How great is the sum of them! If

I should count them, they are more in number than the sand; when I awake, I am still with thee."

When you go to sleep at night, you are in His care—and He is still on duty when you wake up in the morning. What a great way to start the day.

Committing your fears to the Lord, does not, however, give you license to be foolish. Dorothy Fosdick once said, "Fear is a basic emotion, part of our native equipment, and like all normal emotions has a positive function to perform. To be afraid when one should be afraid is good sense."

When the publishing house for which I worked moved to the foothills just outside of Denver, I decided to find a place to live that would be closer to work. This was my introduction to "town house living." There was a certain comfort in having neighbors connected to the walls on both sides of my house.

This feeling, however, was shattered when we started having a rash of break-ins. Seven in all. One evening two homes were hit. Sometimes there would be two, three and even four weeks in between. They could occur at any time of the day or night, but always when the residents were away from home. At the slightest noise, I found myself jumping out of bed in the middle of the night to look out the window. Several times police cars were parked in front, or in a neighbor's carport out back.

In desperation, the managers of our complex invited all of the tenants to meet with the security officers of the Lakewood Police Department. Their instruction and advice put an end to the foolishness of our fear. Sliding patio doors were being easily lifted out of their tracks to give quiet and speedy entry into the townhomes. Front doors were being opened with the aid of a plastic credit card. And I discovered that I was not the only woman alone who had opened her door at the ring of a perfect stranger.

What we learned is worth passing on. Have a security officer from your police department visit your home to check it for safety improvements. Then, hire a reliable lock and key company to install the suggested additions. If your police department does not offer this service, the lock company will be able to help.

I already had a dead bolt lock on my front door, but my sliding doors and windows were vulnerable spots. Key locks were installed on the windows, a board was cut to fit the groove in the sliding door and screws were added to the top of the door so it could not be lifted out.

"Do not, I repeat, do not open your door to any one you do not know," the officer stressed. "Go to the door and ask who it is," he continued, "and if you do not know the person, regardless of their mission, tell them you are busy, or not interested." It is important to answer "through" the door, however, so they will know someone is at home. This was the method used to discover the unattended houses in our complex.

"A well-lighted exterior is the best deterrent to crime," the officer said as he encouraged all tenants to leave front porch and carport lights on all night. I noticed very little increase in my monthly utility bill and only a few tenants out of a total of sixty refused to "light up." Timers set to turn your usual lights on and off inside the house were recommended whenever you plan to be away overnight.

"Neighborhood Watch" is a system sponsored by our local police. It simply means that each neighbor agrees to watch out for others. If you plan to leave town you are to tell the people living on both sides of you. They in turn will let you know if they are to be gone. You don't have to live in a townhouse for this to be effective. It will work any place where there are neighbors. Through this cooperation our "intruder" was apprehended and an end put to our break-ins.

"Operation ID" is another service offered by our Lakewood Police Department. Electric pens are provided for marking appliances, television sets, radios, cameras—anything that might attract a burglar. Your name and zip code are etched on each item and an inventory, with description, is placed on file in the security office of the department. An attractive sticker stating that you are a member of "Operation ID" and that the contents of your house are marked with your identification is placed at all points of entry into your house. Few burglars, we were told, will enter where this sticker is displayed. Having done my part—I turned over and went to sleep!

If your "Mr." did most of the night driving, you may find taking over the wheel, now that you are alone, a fearful necessity. Commit this fear to the Lord—and use a few common sense precautions of your own. The two together will guarantee success. You wouldn't think of jumping off of the Empire State Building at the same time you are praying, "Lord, give me a safe landing." If you run around at night with your car doors unlocked, it amounts to the same thing.

Day, or night, program yourself to automatically lock your car doors when you enter your vehicle—and again when you leave it, even to run into the store for a few minutes. Be sure, however, that the keys are on the outside with you. One day, I found myself looking helplessly in the window at my car keys lying on the front seat. Without a husband to call, this can be a frustrating, if not frightening, experience. I now carry a spare key in my coin purse at all times—just in case.

I used to be very aware that I was alone when driving at night, especially when I had to pull up alongside of another car at a stop light. One night I happened to turn and look at the car next to me. The occupants, all young men, smiled and indicated they wanted to "drag." I smiled back and took off—very slowly. I added a new item to my list of "rules for the road." Don't look at the cars on either side of you. It may call attention to your aloneness and appear to be an invitation. In other words, mind your own business and draw as little attention to yourself as possible.

If you do have to be out in the car alone at night, plan your travel route before leaving home. Avoid deserted streets. Whenever possible take the freeway. There are no traffic lights to stop you and the flow of traffic at the increased speed allows you to become just another car.

I have a fear of running out of gasoline, so I seldom allow my tank to get below the one-quarter mark. If you do have car trouble, or run out of gas, don't leave your car. Turn your emergency blinkers on, keep your doors locked and wait for assistance from the police, or highway partol.

Vi Pearson once drove from Denver to Michigan—alone. She had a delightful time, sightseeing as she pleased, stopping to eat at will and starting out each day as early—or as late—as she felt inclined. The one rule she followed consistently was to stop early enough to get "settled" in a good motel well before dark. I haven't braved cross-country travel by car, but if I ever do, I will follow the same precautions that I do in town—plus a few new ones!

There is a French Proverb that says, "Fear gives intelligence even to fools." An intelligent approach to driving alone is proof of a wise woman.

There are other fears the single person has to fight that have nothing to do with the dark, or physical danger. For example, there is the fear of making decisions. Two people can discuss the pros and cons of an issue and together make a decision. Perhaps we just like having someone to share the blame if it turns out to be the wrong one, but it still helps. "Do you like gold, or green, for the livingroom walls?" How do you decide alone? How can you be sure which will be best? Most of us like to have another person reassure us that we are making a wise decision—or warn us that we are about to make a mistake.

Friends are not the same as a spouse, but in this area they do very well. Deciding to buy a new car wasn't a bit difficult—but what kind was another matter. One of the young men at work took me in tow and pointed me in the right direction and the decision was easy.

More recently, I had to decide on the color carpeting to be installed in my new condominium. Somewhere I got the idea that I would like off-white. It sounded so elegant, feminine—and impractical. Relating my choice to Evelyn Verrill on the phone one day, she responded with, "Are you sure that's what you want? It could be a problem to keep clean." Now, I had doubts.

I took the off-white sample to my office the next day and laid it on the floor for all to see. "It's beautiful, but I wouldn't have it in my house," was the first reaction.

It was also the second and third. I gave a bit more thought to the decision and ended up with a lovely green carpet. These friends didn't make the decision for me, but they kept me from making what might have been a mistake. I really had secret doubts about the white carpet. I feel great about the green.

When God's Word clearly directs you to a "yes" or "no" decision, you need no outside help. That should be enough. Many decisions, however, are between two good things, or your choice may involve a good thing and a better one. Pray that God will give you direction and then watch for Him to use people and circumstance to show you the way.

When I decided to buy a condominium, friends were invaluable in helping eliminate the less desirable ones. After location and structure were approved, however, I was on my own. I drew up a proposal, listing the price I was willing to pay and the changes that would have to be made. I laid it before the Lord and prayed, "If this is Your will for my future, make this offer acceptable to the builder." I knew at that moment I would not be disappointed if it were turned down. It wasn't, and once again I was reassured that my Heavenly Father is concerned about every area of my life.

Pray about decisions—and don't be afraid to seek the advice of friends and/or professionals. You will soon begin to trust your single person decisions and like the feeling of confidence that comes with the package.

Fears come in many sizes and shapes. There are big ones that haunt and little ones that nag. Some work inside out. Others outside in. You may laugh mine off—and I might wonder about yours. But few recently widowed, or divorced, persons can escape having one or two with which to cope.

There is the fear of personal danger; financial responsibility; being alone; being with people, especially couples—and fear of self. David Seabury once said that fear of self is "The greatest of all terrors, the deepest of all dread, the commonest of all mistakes.

From it grows failure. Because of it life is a mockery. Out of it comes despair." Almost every person who has been cut loose from his mate touches base with fear of self. But the wise single begins to discover his own worth and quickly moves on to lesser fears.

We don't have a corner on fear. It has been around for a long time. And God has been telling His children, from the beginning, not to be afraid. When the Israelites were fleeing from Pharaoh, they found themselves with their toes touching the edge of the Red Sea. Pharaoh was barreling down on them with his high-powered chariots—and they were afraid. In Exodus 14:13 and 14, Moses said, ". . . Fear not, stand still and see the salvation of the Lord which he will show you today; . . . The Lord shall fight for you, and ye shall hold your peace."

Three months after the divorce the property settlement was scheduled for a court hearing. Our lawyers had not been able to reach a "mutually acceptable agreement." Ray and I would have to appear. As the dreaded day drew near I had to admit that I wasn't afraid—I was terrified. I found a beautiful portion of scripture that I read every day for a week before the hearing. It is in Deuteronomy 20 as a part of the law of warfare that Moses was delivering to the children of Israel. Here is the last part of verse 3 and verse 4. ". . . Let not your hearts faint, fear not, and do not tremble, neither be ye terrified because of them; For the Lord your God is he who goeth with you, to fight for you against your enemies, to save you."

The Lord did go with me into that court room. My heart did not faint—and I did not tremble. Prior to that day I was afraid of crossing Ray, of standing up to him, and even of hurting him. Had he not remarried before the day of the settlement, I probably would not have been able to hold out against his financial demands. Until then I felt strangely responsible for him. But with God's help I stood and for the first time since the separation—I was free.

David so simply wrote in Psalms 56:3, "When I am afraid, I will trust in thee." This covers all fears—and it works!

Doing Something Different

"Brethren, I count not myself to have apprehended; but this one thing I do, forgetting those things which are behind, and reaching forth unto those things which are before, I press toward the mark for the prize of the high calling of God in Christ Jesus."

Philippians 3:13,14

*V*i Pearson walked into my office one morning shortly after Ray and I had separated. "I have two tickets to the circus for Friday night," she announced. "Would you like to go with me?"

I hadn't been to a circus since Ronnie was a boy—and I wasn't exactly in a circus mood right then, but I knew she didn't just happen to have those tickets. She was prescribing the "do something different" therapy for a friend who was hurting.

We went to the circus—and it was fun. I laughed at the clowns, sat on the edge of my seat as the aerialists performed their feats at breath-taking heights and loved every animal act from the smallest dog to the most enormous elephant. Underneath the hurt was still there, but for that one evening it was less acute.

The "something different" that you do will depend on the circumstances. If you have just lost your loved one by death, no one is going to try to take you to a circus the next week. Down the road a little way there are things you can do that will give you a lift and we'll get to those later. If, however, you have recently been divorced, or find yourself hanging in the state of limbo between separation and decree, you need to do something different—now!

Eating at your favorite little restaurant, having your car serviced at the same station, watching the news on the same channel—or going to bed at precisely the same time that you did when you were married—is a good way to pour salt into those newly inflicted wounds. It's a little like hanging around after the band has stopped playing. You can still remember the tune, but the music is gone. You need to move on, break that routine—get out of that rut.

That trip to the circus was only the beginning. Vi soon had us enrolled in a six-week Stretch and Sew class. I had to work to keep up with each week's sewing assignment. Not long after that project was completed, we signed up for a ten-week seminar on finances. We were going to learn about investments, stocks and bonds. Sitting in that class the first week, I thought, "What am I doing here? I'm strictly a Savings Account-Mutual Funds person." But it was different and interesting. And, it stretched my mind and broadened my understanding.

That first spring, I received a small inheritance from the estate of an aunt, my father's sister, in Sweden. When I called Ronnie to tell him about it, he suggested something really different.

"Mom, why don't you take the money and *go* to Sweden and visit your dad's relatives?"

It wasn't as impossible as it sounded at first. We both knew that Lois and my nephew, Pete, were leaving the first of June to visit Bill who was stationed in Germany. The three of them were planning on driving to Sweden to meet our cousins living there. I was deeply involved in preparation for the court hearing on the property settlement coming up in less than a month. It never crossed my mind that I might be able to go, too. I thought about it for a week, or two, and then placed a call to Phoenix.

"Hi! How would you like company on your trip through

Europe?" I blurted out.

"We'd love it!" Lois quickly replied.

I had just three weeks to get a passport, make reservations, get my work in order—and pack. Fifteen days after "my day in court," I was on a DC-10 bound for New York City, the first lap of my journey. As I settled in my seat on the huge 747 Jet ready for the flight across the ocean, the view from my window was blurred by the tears in my eyes. Here I was, starting out on the most exciting and different experience of my life—and I was alone. My "special person" should have been beside me. Instead, two weeks earlier I had faced him in a court of law to ask for a fair settlement of our joint property. As I saw him that day, the first time in six months, I had to remind myself, "He is someone else's husband now." And it still hurt.

I *needed* something different to do!

My father was born in Sweden, the oldest of a family of nine children. He came to the United States when he was eighteen. He was struck by lightning and killed when I was but six months old. I always felt a little cheated because I didn't know him. Bits and pieces were all that Mother could tell us about his family. One half of our family tree was a mystery. And we were soon to find the answer.

Out of that month we were in Europe, ten days were spent with our family in Sweden. I have never been so completely happy. We met twenty-two new and delightful relatives. We fell in love with them—and their beautiful country.

At the Orly Airport in Paris, France, I left Lois and the boys and boarded another jet for the trip home. Those thirty-one days of escape from the past had done the trick. I felt great. The complete change of scenery had been excellent therapy. The pain cycle was broken.

Now, I realize that you may not have twenty-two un-met relatives in a faraway land, nor the inheritance to make such a trip possible, but the "do something different" principle can be applied closer to home. Is there some part of our country you have always wanted to visit, but never have? Do it. Whether you have lost your mate by death, or divorce, a change of scenery will help.

In many European countries it seemed as if half of the population used bicycles for transportation. Age made no difference. Since I was beginning to enjoy doing something different, I asked Ronnie and Mary, my daughter-in-law, to help me pick out a bicycle. They thought it was a good idea, but I could see that Ronnie was a bit dubious about my biking skills. We decided on a "Free Spirit" three-speed bike. Ronnie put it together when we got home and we all gave it a trial run. Everyone was a bit relieved when we discovered that how to ride a bike is something you don't forget—even after thirty years.

I started riding from two to four miles each evening after work. With the wind in my face, I felt like a kid again—truly a "free spirit." Sometimes the boys next door rode with me, but when I was alone, I found myself singing as I peddled along. Now, that's good medicine for anyone—man, or woman. If you are not already a bike rider—try it.

By fall, Vi no longer had to "sign" me up for something different and we decided to relax and do something not so mind-bending. We settled for a season's ticket to the Denver Symphony—an experience neither one of us had ever taken time to enjoy.

Looking back over that first year, I have to chuckle. It had certainly been packed with variety, In my state of emotional upheaval and adjustment, I would never have thought up these "different" things to do. I was fortunate in having good friends who set out to help. If your friends are more prone to sit and feel sad with you, take the initiative and plan some fun, interesting, challenging and different things to do.

After Bob was killed, it wasn't quite as easy, but each thing we did that was different, seemed to bring a new spark of interest into our lives. Ronnie was taking trombone lessons at the time of Bob's death. Afterwards, he refused to continue. Before long, he indicated an interest in the guitar and we started him on lessons. He still plays the guitar and loves it today.

For me, a paint brush and a can of paint opened the door to change. I changed the color of the outside of the house. I changed the accent color in the kitchen. It was predominately blue and white. There was a strip of molding that went all around the room where the wall and ceiling met. It had a scalloped edge. Bob and I had spent hours, with a water-color brush, painting that scallop red. I decided to make it yellow! Have you ever tried to cover red paint with a lighter color? Three tedious coats later—I had something different.

With the help of a new bedspread, drapes and pictures, I turned the bedroom into a gal's room. It did much to calm the bedroom blues. It gradually became "my" room, instead of "ours." Eventually I replaced our worn-out livingroom furniture and got Ronnie a new full-sized bedroom set. Plans made with Bob were being carried out.

The second year I even tried dating. Well-meaning friends often tried to be matchmakers. I finally agreed to a date with a young man in our church. It turned out that his main interest was stock car racing! The only trouble was, I hated the noise and the pushing crowds. He was poor competition with the memory of Bob.

Then, I decided to take piano lessons. I had never had one in my life. I contacted Lillian Terwilliger, a friend whose musical talent I admired very much. "Lillian, do you think you could teach me to play the piano at my age?" I inquired.

"If you can hobble in on your cane, I'll do my best," she teased.

I rented a spinet piano, with an option to buy, just in case I couldn't hack it. For two years I pursued the field of music in my spare time. I never got beyond the stage of playing for my own amazement, but I will never regret the effort. My teacher once said, "Your mind is quick to grasp the theory, but your fingers are a bit slow to respond."

After the loss of a mate by death, or divorce, it is easier to slide along in your loneliness, just waiting for the miracle of time to do its work of healing. You don't have to do a thing. It's life as usual. Only, life is not the same. It is different. You are different. You are a new individual person.

We could draw a parallel between this change in your life and what happens when a person becomes a new child of God. Paul puts it this way in II Corinthians 5:17, "Therefore, if any man be in Christ, he is a new creation; old things are passed away; behold, all things are become new." A new Christian who refuses to let the old things pass away, will never know the joy of his new life in Christ.

Paul put it another way in Philippians 3:13, 14. "Brethren, I count not myself to have apprehended; but this one thing I do, forgetting those things which are behind, and reaching forth unto those things which are before, I press toward the prize of the high calling of God in Christ Jesus."

Paul had many things in his past life that were best forgotten. He had witnessed and approved the stoning of Stephen; he made havoc in the churches, casting men and women into prison and was guilty of "breathing out threatenings and slaughter against the disciples of the Lord."

And then, one day Paul met Jesus on the road to Damascus. After this experience, he was a different person. He could have spent his life regretting the past, but Paul put the past behind him and reached forth—to the new.

A newly bereaved, or divorced, person who tries to hold onto the past, will find the road to recovery sadly slow. You may be thinking, "That's easy enough to say, but how do you stop the memory computer from automatically recalling the past?" There is a difference between *remembering* the life you had with your "special person" and trying to *live* that life alone.

Right now all of your memories are of the good times, the adventures or discoveries, and the holidays spent with your mate. Doing something different is necessary to feed new experiences into that computer. You will never forget the old memories completely, and you wouldn't want to, but they should be balanced by the new. Don't be afraid to stretch your imagination—and do something different!

After Bob was killed, I went through Easter, Mother's Day, Father's Day and his birthday with the haunting memories of happier days. By the time Thanksgiving rolled around, I realized that we had to find a way of handling holidays that would give us a few fresh memories to recall.

8

Handling Holidays

"Be anxious for nothing, but in everything, by prayer and supplication with thanksgiving, let your requests be made known unto God. And the peace of God, which passeth all understanding, shall keep your hearts and minds through Christ Jesus."

Philippians 4:6,8

I knew we were in for a bad time the evening before Thanksgiving. That big, naked bird almost slipped to the floor as I removed the plastic wrapping. I felt so awkward, but then getting the turkey ready had always been Bob's job. I began to wash it, as I had seen him do every Thanksgiving and Christmas for ten years. The tears began to roll down my cheeks. It was no fun without him!

Brushing the tears away, I breathed a hurried prayer. "Oh, Lord, help me to make tomorrow a good day."

Later that evening with Ronnie tucked into bed and everything possible done for the next day, I curled up with my Bible. Turning to the concordance, I looked up the words "thanks," and "thanksgiving." I knew I had many things to be thankful for, but tonight, I needed reinforcement.

Turning first to Ephesians 5:20, I read, "Giving *thanks* always for all things unto God and the Father in the name of our Lord Jesus Christ."

"All things, Lord? Even Thanksgiving without Bob?" my heart cried.

Next, I flipped the pages back to I Corinthians 15:54-57. "So, when this corruptible shall have put on incorruption, and this mortal shall have put on immortality, then shall be brought to pass the saying that is written, Death is swallowed up in victory. O death, where is thy sting? O grave, where is thy victory? The sting of death is sin; and the strength of sin is the law. But *thanks* be to God, who giveth us the victory through our Lord Jesus Christ."

Victory through Christ. I didn't have to fight the battle alone. Now we were getting someplace. I tried one more reference. Philippians 4:6-8 wrapped it up for me. "Be anxious for nothing, but in everything, by prayer and supplication with *thanksgiving,* let your requests be made known unto God. And the peace of God, which passeth all understanding, shall keep your hearts and minds through Christ Jesus. Finally, brethren, whatever things are true, whatever things are honest, whatever things are just, whatever things are pure, whatever things are lovely, whatever things are of good report; if there be any virtue, and if there be any praise, *think on these things.*"

Ronnie's two grandmas and his aunt and uncle were coming for dinner the next day. They would arrive around 1:00 P.M. It was the early part of the day that we would have to spend alone. I would be busy with the dinner, but how to make the day truly Thanksgiving Day for Ronnie? That last verse I read started me thinking. Suppose I could get him to "think on these things," the things he had to really be thankful for? Better yet, why not have him write them down? But, would he do it? An incentive, that's what he would need.

One look at his face the next morning and I could tell it was already "blue Thursday" for him. While we were eating breakfast, I slipped my plan into the conversation.

"You know, dear, that Thanksgiving is a day to give thanks to the Lord for our blessings. And, we really do have many things for which we can thank Him. So—I'll make a deal with you." Reaching for my props on top of the refrigerator, I continued. "Stick this little note pad and pencil in your pocket. Everytime you think of something you are honestly thankful for, write it down. Number them as you go and at the end of the day I will give you a nickle for each one."

He looked a little dubious, but finally said, "O.K." I wasn't sure it would work, but before long he was taking the pad out of his pocket and carefully writing, "I am thankful for . . ." At the end of the day, he had thirty-seven items on his list. As I read them, I was relieved to find, "I'm thankful for my Mom." I had made number thirty-two! He was $1.85 richer and our whole family day was brightened by his search.

Wearily I crawled into bed. All I could pray was, "Thank you, Father, it *was* a good day."

Our first big holiday hurdle was behind us and Christmas was on its way. I had discovered that we could rise above the holiday blues by making each one a little special. In this way we would be building some good memories to look back on next year. I discussed this with Ronnie and we decided it would be fun, and certainly different, to entertain a couple of orphans in our home on Christmas day. We were going to ask for a boy and a girl.

I called to make the necessary arrangments only to discover that we were not the only ones wanting to share Christmas with one of these children. They were limiting one to each family. Somehow, we thought we had originated the idea, but were happy to learn that it had been going on for years. Mrs. Harris, the lady on the phone, couldn't tell me whether we would have a boy, or a girl, but we were to pick up our "mystery guest" at 10:00 A.M. Christmas morning.

"If we can only have one, I hope it's a boy," Ronnie groaned when I relayed the news to him. At ten years of age, the possibility of a girl guest dampened his enthusiasm a bit. I breathed a prayer for help, for I was counting on this idea to make Christmas special for both of us. Our in-town relatives were limited to my mother, Bob's mother, his sister and her husband. There were no family children close by, with whom he could share holidays.

Promptly at 10:00 A.M. Ronnie and I drove up in front of the orphanage, having left the rest of the family waiting at home. Ronnie was obviously nervous as we sat in the waiting room. I couldn't help wondering myself what the day would bring. My thoughts were interrupted by a whispered, "Oh, no!"

Coming down the hall, headed straight for us, was the skinniest, shiest little black-eyed girl we had ever seen. She was six, or maybe seven years old. It was hard to tell. Mrs. Harris greeted us and then presented our guest. "This is Patty. Patty, this is Ronnie and his mother, Mrs. Ross. You are going home with them for dinner." I don't know who was dreading the day ahead more, Patty or Ronnie.

I chatted away as we drove home, getting little response from Ronnie—and absolutely none out of Patty. When we reached home the rest of the family took Patty in tow and helped her open her gifts. Ronnie headed for his room—and I was not far behind. "Mom," he groaned in despair, "What am I going to do with her all day?"

"I don't really know," I laughed, "but you will think of something. Just remember, we are strangers to her and she is scared to death. *You* are among friends!" I left him alone to think it over. In a few minutes he came out of his room, a determined look on his face.

"Hey, Pat, do you want to go sledding?" I heard him ask. She nodded and reached for her coat.

I heaved a sigh of relief and headed for the kitchen to check on dinner. Everything went along fine. Patty was beginning to enjoy herself. Other kids in the neighborhood joined them and I almost forgot about them. That is, until Patty fell off the sled and narrowly escaped getting run over by a neighbor's car! A shaken boy quickly brought an unharmed, but scared little girl into the house. As soon as possible, I announced dinner.

The near disaster was soon forgotten as the flicker of the red Christmas candles and the sight of the golden brown turkey reminded us that we were starving! I watched Patty as her plate was piled with food. What had her six years of life been like? Had we really brightened her day—or had we used her to take our minds off another Christmas just one year ago, when our little family had been intact? I prayed that we had been successful in doing both.

At 4:00 P.M. we delivered Patty safely back into the hands of Mrs. Harris. As we told Patty goodbye and were about to leave, she looked shyly at Ronnie and said, "Thank you." Back in the car, Ronnie said, "I'm sure glad she didn't get hit by that car." I was, too! The day had been a bit hectic, but it was certainly a Christmas we would never forget.

The New Year slipped in almost unnoticed and February, the month I most dreaded, was just around the corner. One special kind of day per month is about all you can cope with that first year. February, the last of our twelve months, was going to hit us with three; Valentine's Day, my birthday, and—February 25th—the day Bob was killed.

Bob had always remembered the special days in our lives and also many non-special days, with cards, small gifts, or fun surprises. Ronnie had tried very hard this past year to follow his daddy's example. With the help of Bob and Lyda Mosier, he was ready for my birthday, but he almost forgot Valentine's Day. He dashed off to a nearby shopping center and the card he bought still makes me laugh and cry at the same time. I retrieved it from my box of "memories" to share with you. Here's the verse:

Good Luck to You on ST. PATRICK'S DAY
May the luck of the Irish
Lead to happiest heights.
And the highway you travel,
Be lined with GREEN LIGHTS.

Very neatly, he printed this note on the bottom of the card, "Dear Mom, I'm sorry but the Valentines were all gone and I wanted to get you one. I love you. Ronnie." This is one "Valentine" I will always keep!

The second year, we were still lonely for our "special person," but the hurt was now shared with the happy memories of "last year." Our next Christmas, we installed a new tradition that lingers today. Two, or three weeks before Christmas Ronnie and I started making candy; plain fudge, fudge with nuts and with raisins, pink divinity and green divinity, almond brittle and date-nut roll.

We packed and gaily wrapped small boxes with this assortment and on Christmas Eve we delivered them to friends who were alone and shut-ins. We announced our arrival by singing Christmas carols at each door. Our singing wasn't all that great, but we were always welcomed warmly at every home. By the time the evening was over, our hearts were filled with the joy of Christmas, for we always received the greater blessing.

Ronnie—now Ron to everyone but me—and his wife Mary live in Costa Rica where he teaches at two Universities. Mary takes on the beginning education of first graders. It was "my turn" to travel to them for Christmas this past year and I was delighted to see this tradition of sharing being continued in their home. Mary was busy bottling home-made poppy-seed salad dressing, her specialty, and boxing her Christmas cookies to share with friends and others less fortunate at this time of year.

Ronnie made frequent visits to the hospital to cheer a lonely student who was recovering from cancer surgery. Christmas afternoon, he "smuggled" slices of turkey into her room—her Christmas wish. Their spirit of Christmas backfired, however, when they gave their maid a gift of one-hundred colones. She took the money and left town to visit relatives—before she had cleaned the house for the holidays!

Holidays with children in the family do take special care. You may not be attracted to our particular solutions, but find the ones that will appeal to you and your children. Make holidays different and special in some area, while still maintaining the security of past traditions. Do something this year that you and your children will happily remember the next. Holidays are meant to be happy, so don't let grief, or loneliness get the upper hand.

You may be thinking, "That's all well and good—if you have children to share holidays with." And you are absolutely right.

Handling holidays when you are left all alone, is another matter. Though some of the ideas and principles can still be applied.

After Ray and I were separated, my adjustment was quite different. Ray was a gourmet cook. He not only fixed the turkey, he prepared the whole dinner. I set the table and decorated it. Sometimes I was assigned the salad—and always the gravy! After nine years of staying out of his way in the kitchen, I discovered that I had lost all confidence that I *could* cook a holiday dinner.

Just two months after I moved into my duplex, I had to face Thanksgiving. Would I dare try to have dinner at my house? Or, would it be better to sit tight and wait for Mary and Ronnie to invite Mother and me up to Boulder? While I was mulling this decision over in my not-so-confident mind, I learned that at least three people at work would be spending the holiday alone. Before I could weigh the consequences I invited all three, plus Ronnie, Mary and Mother.

I was nervous, but I had a ball. One guest, whose wife had to work all day, remarked, "Amy, I didn't dream you could cook so well!" He had been a guest at several of Ray's special dinners. Though I will never qualify as a gourmet cook, I now have every confidence that I can entertain with ease.

If you are alone, waiting to be invited to share another families' holiday may be depressing. Consider the alternative. Take the initiative and do the entertaining yourself. You will never feel like an outsider in your own home. Nor, will you need to worry that you may have been included out of pity. Being host, or hostess, for awhile at least, is a nice position to hold. You will soon relax and be able to enter the world of give and take in social occasions.

If I had to sum up the solution to handling holidays in one phrase, it would have to be: Force your thoughts to reach out to others, instead of allowing them to be directed inward to self-pity. Start now planning for your next happy holiday!

9

Eating In—or Out

"Commit thy way unto the Lord; trust also in him, and he shall bring it to pass."

Psalms 37:5

*T*o those still a part of the world of couples, eating in, or out, is as normal as breathing. The minute you are "singled," however, it becomes a problem. Not one that can't be solved, but nevertheless—a problem. I'll never forget the feeling I had the first time I walked into a restaurant alone after Ray and I had separated.

"One?" the hostess inquired. I glanced over my shoulder to be sure, and then replied, "Yes, one." It was probably my imagination, but her tone of voice made me want to apologize for even being hungry.

Married people have times when they, too, must dine alone and I doubt if this same question bothers them at all. It is simply an inquiry to determine at what size table they are to be seated. To those who have recently joined the single world, it becomes an indictment.

If you are looking for the easy way out of this problem, you can refuse to enter a restaurant alone—and retreat to the sanctum of your own home for those solo meals. Dining out can be reserved for times shared with friends.

I tried this solution. Fixing breakfast was a breeze. A bowl of soup and a sandwich at night was no real problem. But, if I started to plan a full dinner, I found myself facing the same question. "One?" A potato, scrubbed and wrapped in foil, should not have to stand the heat of that oven alone!

The answer to this, of course, is to invite friends or family in for dinner, and I enjoy this when my busy schedule permits. Many times, however, in self-defense I have to eat out. I had to find a way of doing it without feeling as if I were a second-class citizen.

There is a restaurant which I had frequented for many years. Ronnie and I used to have Sunday dinner there when he was still at home. Later, Ray and I enjoyed dining there on occasion. The first two, or three, times I went alone, the hostess said, "Will someone be joining you?" Or, "Are you dining alone, today?" This didn't last long. She soon accepted the fact that I was certainly alone. I made it a point to be friendly to the waitresses—and to be generous with my tip.

The law of economics dictates that it is more profitable to serve a table of two, four, or more, than it is just one. For this reason, the single person should never tip below the standard—and a little extra can only help.

If you don't have a favorite restaurant where you are known, cultivate one. It helps to have a comfortable haven for times when you are a bit down and need the security of the familiar. Don't get in a rut, however, and be afraid to try a new place to eat.

One Sunday, after church, I stopped at a lovely restaurant not far from the hospital where my mother was recovering from a broken shoulder. Ray and I had eaten there several times, but it had recently changed hands. The way I was received that day started me on a search for ways to combat prejudice against singleness! I decided to accept the rebuffs, the slights, as a challenge. I have to admit that eating out since then has become an adventure.

A heavy, middle-aged man greeted me at the door. "Are you alone?" he asked. When I agreed that I was, he abruptly turned to a waitress nearby and said, "Put her at table eleven with that other woman." Too surprised to object, I meekly followed the waitress to a small table near the kitchen door where an elderly lady was already eating her soup.

The waitress didn't bother to ask if she minded sharing her table, nor did she ask me if I objected to being seated with a stranger. I smiled at the puzzled guest and asked, "Is it all right with you if I sit here?" She assured me it was. What else could she say under the circumstances?

Extremely tired, and with a long afternoon ahead of me at the hospital, I had looked forward to the quiet and solitude of eating dinner alone. Feeling guilty, I asked the Lord to make me a blessing to this little stranger who had just crossed my path. We had a delightful conversation and the time passed quickly. She was a Christian and had just recently lost her husband through death. She lived a block away and walked to this restaurant almost every Sunday. Her husband used to bring her here when he was living.

"I like to sit in one of those booths by the windows, but the new owner always puts me back here," she confided. With just a trace of a tear in her eye, she continued, "I guess he doesn't want to waste a booth on a little old lady."

"Cheer up, dear," I replied, "he didn't want to waste it on me, either."

I had my car and could drive to any restaurant in the city if I wanted to, but this lonely little person could not. My blood began to boil. I wasn't sure what I was going to do, but I had to do something. She was just starting to eat her dessert, when I told her good-by and made my way to the front of the restaurant to pay my bill. The big man seemed happy enough to take my money. Then quite routinely he asked, "Was everything all right?"

Here was my chance. Keeping my voice very low, I began, "The food was delicious, as always, but your treatment of a woman dining alone is rude, inconsiderate and cruel." His mouth fell open. I continued. "Not only did you make me feel unwelcome today, but every week you stick that dear little lady back by the kitchen door." His face turned red. He started to speak, but I beat him to it. "Don't bother to apologize. Just take better care of her—I won't be returning." With that I calmly walked out and I have never been back.

I'm not even suggesting that you run around telling off owners of eating places. I was surprised at myself. But we don't have to take that kind of treatment. What we need is a better way. I was telling this story to my daughter-in-law's father one time and he gave me a couple of pointers that have revolutionized my dining out.

When you eat at a new restaurant, don't accept the first table offered. Instead, say, "Would it be all right if I sit over there?" This puts you in command and shows that you are not apologizing for entering their establishment alone.

If the host, or hostess, hesitates as if trying to decide just where to put you, speak up and ask for a specific location. I decided to give it a try.

A Love's Restaurant opened up not far from my home and I dropped in for dinner one evening. "One?" the hostess asked. I smiled at her and said, "Yes, I'm alone." She hesitated as she tried to decide the best place to put a single. Still smiling, I said, "I'd like that booth over by the window." Taken by surprise, she replied "Come right this way." It had worked!

With a little practice, eating out happily becomes a way of life. I recently had opportunity to test the system again. One Sunday, after church, I decided a short drive was in order. I headed for Littleton, a suburb of Denver, and a delightful family restaurant. I had been there before, but with friends. On Sundays there is always a waiting list. It was a beautiful day and a good-looking young man was standing just outside the door taking names. He greeted me warmly and I said, "One, for Young." He added it to the bottom of the list and I went inside to wait. In just a few minutes he approached me and said, "Would you like to sit at the counter?" Without hesitation, I smiled and with a lilt in my voice, replied, "No, I wouldn't."

Before long, he returned to take me to a choice table that could easily have handled four.

Two weeks later I went back. When I announced, "One, for Young," he smiled and said, "Nice to have you back, Mrs. Young." This time there was no mention of the counter.

The secret of success is your attitude. Go in with your head up and a pleasant look on your face. If you become irritated when asked to sit at the counter, you have lost the battle. What you really want is a good dinner in a welcome atmosphere. To be in control of your dining destiny, you must exhibit more poise than all of the hosts and hostesses in town.

One of the worst things you can do is to walk into a restaurant with "rejection" written all over you. Or, with "I'm unimportant" pinned to your lapel. It will be the table by the kitchen door, for sure, if you do. If you have avoided eating out alone, give this system a try. It is excellent therapy when you are a bit on the dreary side of life. It is fun to watch for the different reactions and at the same time your self-esteem and confidence will grow by leaps and bounds.

Now that you are seated at a good table and the waiter has taken your order, what do you do while you wait? Where do you look? Do you stare at the water glass, the ceiling, or worse yet, the floor?

When Vi Pearson dines alone, she takes something to read. I am a people-watcher. I study people, try to guess what they do for a living and who's who in the family lineup. I'm also an avid eavesdropper. Some interesting bits of conversation drift your way. All are not worth listening to, but you soon learn to tune the dull ones out and the lively ones in, much as you do stations on the radio dial.

Several times, recently, I have noticed a particular man dining alone at my favorite restaurant. Applying my people watching technique, I tried to discover what method he used to entertain himself. He was different. He didn't have anything to read and he was certainly no people-watcher. Except to place his order, his eyes never left the table in front of him. He could have been eavesdropping, but that's difficult to do without an occasional glance at the people talking. I concluded that he was a day-dreamer. A diner lost in his own thoughts. It doesn't matter what system you use—just what makes you the happiest and most comfortable.

Dining out with married couples can also require a bit of adjustment. In the early stages of your recovery, "Three?" or, "Five?" can be as hard to cope with as "One?" Being that fifth wheel makes you very aware that your "special person" is not by your side. How to pay your share of the check can also be awkward, if not a real problem.

I eat out frequently with Maxine and Ed, two of my closest friends. We have a good system. Sometimes, they will say, "We are taking you out for dinner tonight." And on occasion I tell them, "Tonight, I'm treating." But most of the time, we go "Dutch." We add the tip to the total bill and divide it by three. We may have to use a pencil to figure it out, but we never let that bother us. The secret is in the understanding you have with your friends. Don't wait until the check arrives to discuss how it is going to be paid. Except on special times, pay your own way.

Nobody likes to eat out all of the time. This brings us to eating alone—at home. When you first find yourself facing meal time alone, it can be a depressing, lonely experience. It doesn't have to last. Let me share some of the things I do to chase away the dinner-time blues.

I bought a cheery, round metal tray. It is bright yellow with red cherries around the edge. A colorful napkin, or a pretty paper towel, becomes my "tray cloth." I set the tray instead of the table. It's much cozier than that seven-foot harvest table! When the weather is warm, I carry it out on the patio and eat at the picnic table. Even for breakfast. I also couple my daily devotions with breakfast. This starts my day off right in more ways than one.

If you are tempted to skip breakfast rather than eat it alone, try these ideas. Set the table, or your tray, the night before. Have your orange juice mixed and waiting in the refrigerator, or pre-section your grapefruit and cover it with plastic, or foil wrap. If it is cereal for the day, place the box by your bowl, or near your tray. Occasionally, use your best dishes and your finest glassware. A single blossom from your flower garden can add a special touch when placed in a bud vase and added to your tray.

With this nightly preparation, you won't dare walk out of the house, or the kitchen, ignoring that pre-set breakfast and that cheery box of cereal. And when you cherish this quiet time in the early hours of the day—you are well on your way to recovery.

For me, lunch is almost always eaten out with friends from work. Two or three evenings a week, I have dinner out. On the nights when I do eat at home, I return to that round tray. I usually eat at the kitchen counter, perched on a high stool. This is an excellent place to spread out and read the evening newspaper. I almost always end up working the daily crossword puzzle. Some-times, the news on TV, or one of the game shows, keeps me company, or if I'm having trouble finding time to finish a book, I'll resort to Vi's remedy and read while I eat.

Eating in, or out, when you are alone need not remain a problem. If my solutions are not right for you, dream up some of your own. Eating is something we usually do three times a day and that is too often to give in to any problem.

Eating in, or out, when you have children at home is an entirely different ball game—and is definitely more fun. You don't have to face that question of "One?" when dining out. And, if on occasion you do eat alone at home, it may be a welcome breather.

After Bob was gone and the Mosiers were settled in their new home, Ronnie and I decided it would be more fun to eat out on Sunday after church than to come home for dinner. Sometimes we went with friends, but many times we were alone. Our first favorite place to eat was a little Italian restaurant. The specialty of the house was Chicken Tetrazzini. It was served piping hot with the rich cheese sauce bubbling up through the homemade spaghetti and generous pieces of chicken. There never was, nor ever will be, any other to equal it.

When Ronnie was about twelve years old, we discovered The Copper Kitchen. We disagreed on their "specialty." For him it was the Golden Fried Shrimp and for me, the Barbecued Chicken. It was during this time that I discovered that to a young boy there is no such period as "between meals." Ronnie could eat a full course dinner plus part of mine and head straight for the refrigerator five minutes after we reached home.

These Sunday dinners were special. We talked and talked—about anything and everything. I also used them as "basic training" for the years ahead when "girl friends" would appear on the scene. Social graces that he would have learned from his dad, would have to be taught by his mom.

We started with checks and tips. Before we reached the restaurant, I gave Ronnie more than enough money to cover our dinners and the tip. At first, the waitresses smiled over his head as he figured the tip—after checking their figures on the bill. Paying and tipping soon became a natural routine.

We moved from money to car doors and restaurant doors. Car doors were easy, but it's quite a trick to be in the right place at precisely the right moment when a restaurant door needs to be opened. A few pointers and a little practice and he was soon handling it like a pro.

We talked about girls—how they should be treated and the kind of behavior that would earn him their respect. When he was half way between fourteen and fifteen, Ronnie discussed with me one Sunday at dinner his viewpoints on how to treat a girl. He later wrote them out and gave me a copy. They are worth repeating.

How To Treat a Girl

1. Be the strong, silent type, but not too silent.
2. Crack as many jokes as possible.
3. Always be clean all over.
4. Brush teeth two times a day.
5. Try to always have hair combed.

6. Be the stronger hand about decisions, but
   be very understanding and fair.
7. Be romantic, but not fresh.
8. Be protective, but don't act tough.
9. Always dress as well and neat as possible.
10. Don't ignore her, but make her miss you by
    not being around all the time so she won't
    get tired of you.

Dining out with your children can be much more than a time to eat. Without the work of preparing the meal and cleaning up afterwards, you should be relaxed and ready to enjoy these offspring of yours. It's a great time for sharing and communication. And for you, the listening half of communication can often be most profitable.

Eating at home should also be special. We found our kitchen at home the best room in the house for talk. Ronnie's duties were to set the table and to dry the dishes. By the time he was grown I had a case of "tired ears," but I wouldn't take a million dollars in exchange for those hours spent listening to anything he had to say.

Eating in, or out, is fun when you have children. It can also be a happy experience even if you are alone.

10

Friends—The Right Mix

"Ye are my friends, if ye do whatever I command you. Henceforth I call you not servants; for the servant knoweth not what his lord doeth: but I have called you friends; for all things that I have heard of my Father I have made known unto you."

John 15:14,15

*W*alter Winchell once said, "A real friend is one who walks in when the rest of the world walks out."

Leafing through the pages of my diary, covering the days after the divorce, I found recorded evidence of friends who had walked into my life to help fill the void when Ray walked out.

March 2
Vi went with me to Hess Jewelers. Had my rings cut off. No point in wearing them now. Wish the hurt would go away. Couldn't help thinking, "What God hath joined together, let not man (cut) asunder." When I told Vi this, she said, "I knew that was going through your mind."

March 9

Heard today that Ray had remarried. Guess I knew it would happen someday—but didn't expect it so soon. It really hit me hard. Still, "All things work together . . ."

March 10

Woke up a 4:15 and couldn't get back to sleep. Cried, prayed—and hurt. Got up about 7:20 to get ready for work, but the tears just wouldn't stop. Decided to stay home. Vi came and took me up to Heritage Square for lunch. Maxine came over to spend the evening. Talked to the Verrills later. The Lord has given me many wonderful friends.

March 11

Went over to Audrey and Teddy's for dinner. Had nice evening. To bed about midnight. So tired.

Two weeks after the divorce was final and over a month before the property settlement, I made this entry in my diary.

March 13

Back to work and setting out to "forget" Ray. How do you just forget nine years of your life? Guess I'll find out. Vi and I stopped at the Farm Kitchen for a bite to eat on our way to sewing class. Alpaca sweaters tonight.

I have another dear friend who has the gift of writing just the right words at the right time. Here is one of her notes.

Dear Amy,

I have been conscious the last few days that you are going through "something." In fact, Amy, last night as I was praying, I became terribly burdened to pray for you, and as I did, I also had an inexplainable weeping session.

Then I thought of the words—the second verse to "Blest Be the Tie that Binds":

"We share our mutual woes
Our mutual burdens bear
And often for each other flows
A sympathizing tear."

I'm not offering you pity or mere sentimental sympathy (in case it's forthcoming). I'm just saying that I *care* and if something hurts you, I want to be sensitive to it and at least stand with you in prayer.

Love,
Edith

These friends and many others were sensitive to my needs and my hurt. I didn't have to say a word, or draw them a picture. They just knew. Vi knew that she could interrupt the heartache of that day with lunch in the foothills of Denver. Maxine knew that evening would be long—and came to help shorten it. Audrey knew that a night out would be good medicine. The words of encouragement from the Verrills and the prayers of Edith and others helped me through those difficult hours.

Everyone needs friends. But as a formerly married single, you need more than that. You need the right mix of friends. What is "right" may differ between individuals, but I believe there is a basic pattern in the life of Christ that is worth considering. First, He was in complete harmony with His Heavenly Father—*and at peace with Himself.* You've heard people say, "He's his own worst enemy." When everything is right between me and my Lord, I find it easy to like myself—to be a friend to me. This is the place to start.

Then Jesus had a group of *good friends.* Their names are given in Matthew 10:2-4.

"Now the names of the twelve apostles are these: the first, Simon, who is called Peter, and Andrew, his brother; James, the son of Zebedee, and John, his brother; Philip and Bartholomew, Thomas and Matthew, the tax collector; James the son of Alphaeus, and Lebbaeus, whose surname was Thaddaeus; Simon the Canaanite, and Judas Iscariot . . ."

These men were a part of His everyday life. He loved them and except for one, they returned this love. He explains the nature of His relationship with them in John 15:14-15. "Ye are my friends, if ye do whatever I command you. Henceforth I call you not servants; for the servant knoweth not what his lord doeth: but I have called you friends; for all things that I have heard of my Father I have made known unto you." These were friends with whom he could communicate openly and freely. He enjoyed their company—they had a common bond.

You, too, should have a group of good friends. The number is not important, but the right mix is. Mine include other singles, some delightful young couples, some older people I have known since childhood—and many couples in my own age bracket. I may see them every day, once a month, or once a year. We may go to different churches, live in different cities, but these good friends are essential to a well-adjusted, happy life.

I have such a friend who holds a rather unique place in my life. She is single, goes to a different church, is years younger than I am and has a different circle of close friends. I see her each day when I arrive at work. Shortly after Sally came to work at the publishing house, we discovered we had a common bond. Our approaching divorces were scheduled for hearing on exactly the same day, hers in the morning, and mine in the afternoon.

As the years clicked off, Sally and I compared notes on the progress of our recovery and encouraged each other on those down days. If our busy lives permit we try to go out to dinner on our "anniversary." This year we almost forgot! We decided that was a good sign.

If you find a friend who is walking the same road that you are be sure you are a help to each other. If it is a case of "misery loving company," you will be better off without such a friend.

Out of the twelve good friends that Jesus had, He chose three to be his *close friends.* They were Peter, James, and John. He had a special rapport with them. He could share His innermost thoughts, most personal experiences and His heaviest burdens. Mark 9:2-4 and 7-10a, give a beautiful example of this relationship.

"And after six days Jesus taketh with him Peter, and James, and John, and leadeth them up into an high mountain, apart by themselves; and he was transfigured before them. And his raiment became shining, exceedingly white like snow, as no fuller on earth can whiten them. And there appeared unto them Elijah with Moses; and they were talking with Jesus.

"And there was a cloud that overshadowed them: and a voice came out of the cloud, saying, This is my beloved Son; hear ye him. And suddenly, when they had looked round about, they saw no man any more, except Jesus only with themselves. And as they came down from the mountain, he charged them that they should tell no man what things they had seen, till the Son of man were risen from the dead. And they kept that saying to themselves . . ."

This was an experience that could be shared only with Jesus' closest friends—those He could trust to honor His request for silence. It would be impossible to draw a parallel between this experience and any that we might have. But, you too, need close friends who can share those precious moments, too beautiful to make public, or too private to lay bare for all to see.

In between the last supper and His arrest, Jesus again chose these three close friends to be with Him. This time to share a burden. The account is recorded in Matthew 26:36-38. "Then cometh Jesus with them unto a place called Gethsemane, and saith unto the disciples, Sit here, while I go and pray yonder. And he took with him Peter and the two sons of Zebedee, and began to be sorrowful and very depressed. Then saith he unto them, My soul is exceedingly sorrowful, even unto death; tarry here, and watch with me."

He told them how heavy His heart was—and they fell asleep. It was not possible for them to understand His need for companionship on that night, but I believe He wanted them there even if they slept.

You need close friends to walk with you through heartache and trouble, but don't ever expect them to grieve as long as you do, or to hurt as deeply. Be thankful that they are standing with you, but don't expect the impossible.

Jesus had three close friends and nine, less one, good friends, but He also had a larger group of friends. They are mentioned in Luke 10:1. "After these things the Lord appointed other seventy also and sent them two by two before his face into every city and place, where he himself would come."

He had fellowship and companionship with His good friends, and intimate sharing with His close friends. Now we see a climate of service within the larger circle of friends. These friends are identified as a group. Nowhere are their names listed and yet as a group they were serving the Lord.

You need an outlet for service. A larger group of people with whom you can identify, fellowship with and together serve the Lord. My "group" is one of the adult Sunday School classes in my church. The average attendance is around 150 each week. The youngest member is in high school and the oldest is in his eighties. There are singles, and couples of all ages in between. They meet a special need in my life. I am the Activities Director and for that size class with that age span—it is a challenge.

I still don't know everyone's name, but I love them in the Lord and have a wonderful sense of belonging. Close friends and good friends are important, but don't overlook the benefits of group friends. This same formula, or friendship-mix, can be applied to anyone's life. But it is especially important for the person who has lost a mate by death—or divorce.

Your close friends should also be of the right mix. Since there seems to be an abundance of single women and few available men, I am going to direct the suggested mix to the gals. It will, however, work as well for the men.

Your close friends should include a single woman. She should be someone who understands you, shares common interests and is free to go places with you at the drop of a hat. She is a pal and a confidante. And unlike her male counterpart, there are no strings attached.

At this point you may be expecting me to suggest a gentleman friend for that inner circle. Since we are dealing with recovery from a broken heart, or a wounded ego, I'm not. If you rebuild your life as a single person to the place that you can say, "I'm happy," then you have something to offer in the romance department. Don't try to heal the hurt of losing your "special person" by replacing him. Heal first. You will be capable of making a wiser choice if you do.

I would not like a totally woman world. I like men. They are usually more interesting to talk with than women, and I like the way their minds work. So for a well-balanced mix in your inner circle, you need at least one married couple. These are not chosen—they are Heaven sent. The woman has to be so secure in her marriage that she doesn't mind, on certain occasions, sharing her husband. I am especially blessed in this area. Maxine and Ed Dannenberg, two of my favorite people, just accept me as one of the family. If I need a manly chore done around the house, Maxine is always quick to say, "Ed will be glad to do that." And he really is.

Every two or three years, we take our vacations together. I would do anything in the world for them and they would do the same for me. This comfortable relationship is expressed in a note I received from Maxine not too long ago.

> Dear Amy,
>
> Just a short note to thank you for the nice birthday dinner last Sunday. It was lots of fun even though it was a rainy day.
>
> Love,
Maxine
>
> P.S. Ed enjoyed the dinner, too. Isn't he lucky to know us and have *two* girl friends? Especially one who takes him out to dinner. Ha!

Close friendships are never one-sided. As a single person you will often be on the receiving end, but you also have the joy and responsibility of sharing a close friend's happiest moments—and his most tragic. It is this two-way sharing that forms that inner circle.

Close friends know you—and love you in spite of your faults. Most of the time they don't even notice. They are constant, never wavering in their friendship—and always there when you need them. The newly singled person who has such friends will find it easy to build a rich, full life.

If, however, you limit yourself and your activities to one, or two, close friends you risk becoming too dependent. This can smother any relationship. Keep a proper balance between those dear close friends, your good friends and that larger group of friends.

Proverbs 18:24 offers some good advice. "A man who hath friends must show himself friendly; and there is a friend who sticketh closer than a brother."

If you do not have the right mix of friendships begin today to do something about it. Be a friend to someone who needs one.

11

Facing Finances

"But my God shall supply all your need according to his riches in glory by Christ Jesus.

                                          Philippians 4:19

*M*oney, or the lack of it, has been the subject of many a quip and a quote. John Gay once said of money:

> *Like Heav'n, it bears the orphans' cries,*
> *And wipes the tears from widows' eyes.*

It isn't, however, quite that easy. It takes more than money to heal the heartache and dry the tears that come from the loss of a mate, but the absence of financial worry does make the burden easier to bear. If money is no problem, the manner of living to which you have become accustomed need not change. There are also certain decisions you will not have to make. You don't have to sell your house unless you want to. You need not look for a job, or decide if the one you already have will be adequate to meet expenses.

There are, however, some drawbacks to having all the money needed. As one recently widowed friend put it, "There is no reason to get up in the morning. There is nothing I absolutely have to do." If you find yourself facing each day with this feeling—get something to do! Commit yourself to a schedule. It may be volunteer work at a hospital, a nursing home, your church office, or whatever, but get busy. With, or without money, the happiest people in the world are those with a job to do.

Having money is a responsibility. If your "special person" handled all financial matters, you need to be very cautious as you take over the checkbook, the bank statement and those stock certificates. Money and sense do not always travel together. Many a newly singled person has fallen for the smooth line of a con artist, or tried to drown their sorrows by reckless spending. Slow down. Seek legal advice, professional counsel—walk lightly until you fully understand your financial picture.

Since death and divorce do not consider a person's financial position, there are many people who have to face a lack of funds right along with their heartache. After death or during divorce, your thinking processes are not at their best. Perhaps some of the financial situations I faced will help you if you are right in the middle of either of these traumas.

I was working when Bob was killed but planned to quit in three months. The new car my paycheck was buying would be "ours" by then and Ronnie would be out of school for the summer. I had worked off and on during the ten years of our marriage, but we had never allowed our standard of living to depend upon my extra income.

Our financial background had been rather simple. We allowed ourselves only one installment payment at a time—and we didn't even own a credit card. Bob usually paid the monthly bills and I only had to cope with the grocery money. Now I was going to have to take over a new house, a nine-year-old boy and all that the two implied—with a salary that was less than half of what Bob's had been.

The first financial decision that had to be faced was how much to spend for the funeral. Bob didn't have a large amount of insurance, so I was forced to be careful. Looking back, I realize that if I had had ten times the amount of insurance that I did, it would still have been wise to select a modest funeral plan.

Sad to say, but some funeral directors take advantage of people when they have little resistance and try to sell them far more than they can afford. Take a friend with you who can be objective about the cost and heed their advice. Don't try to show your love for that "special person" by spending money you will need for the future. He, or she, would not want you to.

The second financial matter to be handled was how to use the balance of the insurance money. A policy for a little over $1,000 went to Bob's mother to repay money borrowed towards the down payment on our house. What was left went into the bank as a buffer fund.

Fortunately, we had mortgage insurance on the car, so it was automatically paid off. We had an appointment to see about mortgage insurance on the house—one week too late. The insurance company representing the man who hit Bob paid $5,000 as settlement. It seemed such a small sum in exchange for our "special person." Feeling the weight of the mortgage on the house—with only three payments made against it—I made a hasty decision. I refinanced the house, applying the entire $5,000 to the loan. If I had it to do over I would not have tied it up that way. It would have been wiser to invest it where it could have grown, and still been available. Some of the financial strain of the next few years would have been eased.

Having money in your pocket and deciding where to spend it is one thing, but a hand full of bills that need paying is quite another matter. Making my income match the outgo suddenly became a challenge. Enter—my first budget book.

My income turned out better than I had first feared. Not only did I get a raise, but Bob's Social Security benefits provided a monthly check for Ronnie that would continue until he was eighteen years of age.

In case you are facing financial responsibility for the first time, let me introduce you to the simple system I started years ago—and still use today. I began by listing every financial commitment I had. First, the monthly bills and living expenses and next, those payments that roll around once or twice a year. Since I got paid on the first and the fifteenth of each month, the monthly expenses needed to be equally divided between these two paydays. I also needed to be reminded of those once a year payments well in advance of their due date so I could be ready for them.

I bought a standard 9x7-inch, three-ring binder; 8½x5½-inch ruled ledger paper and two 9x6-inch manila envelopes punched to fit the notebook. The first page covered the yearly expenses and looked something like this:

YEARLY EXPENSES		
Item	Due Date	Amount
Car License	January	90.00
Car Insurance	5/12	280.00
Homeowner's Insurance	9/24	98.00
Income Tax Service	4/15	35.00

By listing these in the front of your budget book you can plan ahead and include them in the proper month for payment.

Here is the next step. Right after your "Yearly Expenses" place a divider marked "Payment Schedules." In this section place a page for each month left in the current year. At the beginning of each new year prepare your schedules ahead for all twelve months. You may have to adjust some of them down the road, but this advance planning gives excellent guidance when new expenditures are considered.

Unless your list of monthly expenses is extremely long you can get both schedules on one page. Here is what a typical page might look like:

January 1 Item	Amount
Tithe	$
House Payment/Rent	$
Telephone	$
Groceries/Lunches/Cash	$
Insurance	$
Doctor	$
TOTAL	

January 15	
Tithe	$
Utilities	$
Groceries/Lunches/Cash	$
Gasoline	$
Savings Account	$
Pharmacy	$
TOTAL	

Work with these expense items until each total is about equal. Then tie them down for that specific payday. Check them off as you write your checks. Your list could include a car payment, charge accounts, loan payments and a number of other items. The secret is to get them all down in black and white. And then face them head-on. You may find that your life style will have to change for a time—until your income exceeds the outgo.

You may prefer to work with a more detailed budget with allowances for clothing, education, vacations, etc. Your family responsibilities will determine this. As a woman alone, I like the guidelines of a monthly payment schedule with the freedom of choice on any amount left over.

An automatic payment into a savings account is a regular monthly budget item. I depend on this for emergencies, vacations, and certain cash purchases. You can authorize your bank to transfer on a given date a definite amount from your checking account into a savings account. This cash reserve is a must for the single person.

Those two manila envelopes are to hold your monthly statements until payday. Mark one the "1st" and the other the "15th."

Some years later I added another section to my budget book. The first part is practical—this one is fun. It is labeled "Record of Progress." I have a page for the record of my tithe. Each payday I enter the check number and the amount. At the end of each year I have an instant total for my income tax reports. It also helps keep me consistent in my giving.

I have another page for that automatic savings account. At a glance I can watch it build. I include interest earned and again it is available at tax time. Right now I enjoy watching the balance decline on another page as I pay for my new car. I am a record keeper. Charting my weight is a recent addition to my budget book. My son's reaction to this was, "Who but my mother would think of keeping a graph of weight gained or lost?" I enjoy my budget book—or my *record* book. But more than that it lets me know at all times where I stand financially. If you don't have a plan for controlling your finances, try this one, or another. Having a plan takes the fear out of facing finances alone.

Finances related to losing a mate by death and divorce are quite different. After death you either have enough to live on, or you have to find a way of making it on your own. The circumstances are usually predetermined.

In the case of divorce the end result is the same. You either have enough to live on, or you have to find a way of making it on your own. The big difference is that this is not predetermined. There are so many variables it would be impossible to uncover them all. Often children are involved with the question of child support. Health and age can be a factor in determining need. The length of the marriage enters the picture. The financial assets of both parties at the time of marriage may make a difference.

All of these can be neatly classified as "cold, hard facts." But there are also less tangible aspects that come to the surface. Attitudes and motives. Does the father *want* to help support his children? Is the wife out to *take* her ex-husband for everything he has? Mix all of the possible motives in with the feeling of being rejected, unloved, unwanted, and you might ask, "Is it possible to be fair?" I believe, with the Lord's help, it is. When Ray walked into the house and announced that he had been to see his lawyer and told me when the papers would be served, I had no idea how our property would, or should, be divided. Within a few days, Ray had drawn up those two lists of furniture and household items. At the bottom of my list was this sentence, "I agree to a 50-50 settlement of all money and property." He asked me to sign it.

Somewhere in the back of my mind, a still small voice warned, "Don't sign anything until you are sure it is the thing to do."

I quietly answered, "I'll have to ask my lawyer, first." I wanted to be fair and I didn't want to hurt Ray, but my lawyer and close friends kept reminding me that I should wait for the court to decide what was fair. It was wise advice and I pass it on to you. Don't rush into decisions. Don't sign anything without legal counsel.

Months later as Ronnie and I sat outside the courtroom, I asked, "Honey, do you think I should agree to their demands?" He replied, "Mom, it's no time for Christmas presents." When the judge announced his decision an hour later, I was thankful for a Christian lawyer, a wise son and Psalms 138:8: "The Lord will perfect that which concerneth me. Thy mercy, O Lord, endureth forever; . . ."

Several days later I held in my hand a check. It was my share of the cash settlement. What should I do with it? Did I want another house with the responsibilities of a yard? My self-confidence was still a bit shaky and I could not reach a conclusion. I decided to put the money in a one-year time deposit and reconsider the house question at that time.

Sally faced the same decision and after a year or so, bought a townhouse. I admired her decisiveness, but still hesitated. While she enjoyed her new home and the tax advantages of owning over renting, I waited. It took me four years to get up enough courage to remove my nest egg, my security blanket, from the bank and buy a condominium.

Don't jump before you know what is right for you and your future. Like Sally, you may know in a year, or like me, in four. Either way, Psalms 37:4-5 is the promise to claim: "Delight thyself also in the Lord, and he shall give thee the desires of thine heart. Commit thy way unto the Lord; trust also in him, and he shall bring it to pass."

Facing finances can be rough when you are alone, but your Heavenly Father knows what you need before you even ask. Give Him first place in your life—and your finances.

12

How to Belong to Your Church

"And let us consider one another to provoke unto love and to good works, Not forsaking the assembling of ourselves together, as the manner of some is, but exhorting one another, and so much the more, as ye see the day approaching."

Hebrews 10:24,25

*D*o the people in your church accept you as a divorced person?" a friend recently inquired.

"No," I replied. "They accept me as another Christian who loves the Lord."

That question started me thinking. I'm sure there are churches today who do pull in the welcome mat when a newly singled adult appears at their doors. Many books and articles are written relating personal experiences that bear out this fact. Divorced persons have been embarrassed, rejected, barred from service and even been asked to produce the divorce decree to prove the reason for the divorce.

This is sad. I'm thankful that I have not found this to be true in my life. I feel loved, respected, supported and welcome. If I did not—I would quietly steal away and look for a church who would welcome me with open arms in Christian love.

Not long ago I read, "It is the church's responsibility to make a place for the formerly marrieds in the church."

Wrong.

At least I don't want a "place" made for me where I am set apart as if I were some unusual species requiring special treatment. I want to *belong* to my church. The whole church. Not just a "place" in it.

You may be asking, "What about the churches who do make a place for the formerly marrieds?" Fine. I have nothing against such a class or group as long as the newly singled person doesn't use it to hide from the rest of the membership. Enjoy the fellowship of such a group—and then go beyond it to serve in some area of your church as an individual. If your singles group meets in the evening, then serve in one of the children's departments in the Sunday School. Or, perhaps the choir would be the place for you to make a contribution. You really belong when you find your place of service.

There is real danger in being uncommitted. Bob and I had both been active in our church and after he was gone I returned to my responsibilities as Superintendent of the Junior High Department in the Sunday School. I wasn't sure I could go it alone, but as I look back I realize it was the best thing in the world I could have done. It goes back to needing a reason for getting up in the morning— even on Sunday. Without that reason it is easy to fall into the devil's trap and end up going " when I feel like it." I found myself in this position after Ray and I separated.

About three or four years before the divorce, Ray and I left the church where Bob and I had served and where Ronnie grew up, in an effort to find a church that would be "ours." That first Sunday when I sat alone, I found my eyes being drawn to the fourth pew from the front where we had sat together on Sunday mornings. After a few sad Sundays, I decided to make a change.

For the next two or three months, I visited different churches—when I wasn't too tired! It is an easy habit to slip into when you live alone. It's a little like leaving the bed unmade if you want to. There is no one to know—or care. And yet, we know there is. Our Heavenly Father does both. The Lord was very close during these days of heartache and emotional adjustment so I wasn't running from Him. I was avoiding close contact with people!

One morning God prodded me into facing something I already knew. I was reading in the tenth chapter of Hebrews when I came to verses 24 and 25. "And let us consider one another to provoke unto love and to good works, Not forsaking the assembling of ourselves together, as the manner of some is, but exhorting one another, and so much the more, as ye see the day approaching."

The next Sunday I returned to my old church. It was like coming home. There was one big difference. I was now a divorcee and I wasn't sure how I would be received. I decided to find out. I called and made an appointment for an interview with Dr. Earle Matteson, the pastor. I had been alone for three months and still had two to go before the divorce would be final. My wounds were still too fresh to risk the additional pain of rejection by fellow Christians.

That hour with this dear man of God put my fears to rest and furnished the reassurance of a Christian welcome and a place of service. He helped me see that my standing in Christ as a child of God was far more important than my position as a divorced person. I was carrying an unnecessary burden.

Whether you are alone as a result of death, or divorce, the need for Christian fellowship and service within the framework of a local church is the same. Alone is alone, no matter how you arrived there. In either case, don't let yourself withdraw from people. Find a warm Bible-believing church with the welcome mat out. Talk to the pastor. Tell him what has happened to you and how you feel about it. It will clear the air of doubts and questions and let you turn your back on the past and walk into the future with a spring in your step—and your head up.

I heard one divorced person complain, "My church does not allow a divorced man to serve on the deacons board." Let's face it. Many churches do have this policy based on I Timothy 3:12: "Let the deacons be the husbands of one wife, ruling their children and their own houses well." A great number of other churches and pastors have restudied the question and feel this requirement has to do with the practice in the culture of that day of taking several wives. These churches will allow divorced and remarried men to serve if they meet the spiritual requirements of Acts 6:3: "Wherefore, brethren, look among you for seven men of honest report, full of the Holy Spirit and wisdom, whom we may appoint over this business."

Right or wrong, my church will probably never ask me to serve as a deaconess. And, do you know I don't even mind. There are many areas of service for which I am not qualified. With my singing voice, I will never be asked to sing in the choir, either. So if there are two or three restrictions, don't feel sorry for yourself. Find a place of service where you do have what it takes and get busy.

I believe the stigma of divorce is much less today than it was even a few years ago. It is a fact of life—of many lives—and our not liking it and all of the theologians in the world's disapproval of it is not going to make it vanish. By the overwhelming number of divorces occurring each year the church is being forced to minister to the needs of the individuals involved.

It is my church's responsibility to accept me for what I am, not for what has happened to me. It is my responsibility to be the kind of a Christian and church member that will be a credit to that church and to my Lord. When you have reached this point in your recovery you will truly belong to your church.

There is one problem that needs to be faced. Since we can never see ourselves as others see us, it is difficult to recognize this problem, except in retrospect. It is summed up in this question asked by an attractive young widow several months after the loss of her husband. "Why is it that the men at church are so much friendlier to me than the women?" I tried to explain.

From the beginning of time, men were meant to take care of women. God gave them a natural instinct and ability to protect the weaker sex. The men in any group will usually rally to the aid of a newly widowed woman. If she was a part of a happy marriage, she misses the attention and companionship of her "special person." She can without even realizing it, accept and encourage this attention by her conduct. While the men are overcome with sympathy for her, their wives back away.

After Bob was gone, the men in the church did rally, and with few exceptions so did their wives. But those few taught me a valuable lesson. A wise friend took me aside one day and gave me some good advice. "Amy, you are as friendly as a puppy dog and you have never met a stranger. That's fine, but watch that wink."

Until that moment I was completely unaware that I even had a wink. After a little investigation, I discovered it was automatically wired to my smile. I disconnected it and was happy to find that I could smile just as well without it. For the first time since Bob was gone, I began to understand that my conduct and the way I expressed my personality were of utmost importance to my Christian walk.

The fifth chapter of Ephesians tells us how we are to walk as believers. In the second verse Paul instructs us to ". . . walk in love . . ." The eighth verse tells us to ". . . walk as children of light." Verses 15-17 were included expecially for you and me.

"See, then, that ye walk circumspectly, not as fools but as wise, Redeeming the time, because the days are evil. Wherefore, be ye not unwise but understanding what the will of the Lord is." It is not hard to understand about walking in love. Love for our Lord and for other Christians. Even walking in the light indicates that it is the opposite of walking in the dark. Psalm 119:105 says, "Thy word is a lamp unto my feet, and a light unto my path." In John 8:12 Jesus said, ". . . I am the light of the world; he that followeth me shall not walk in darkness, but shall have the light of life.

But what about circumspectly? From Ephesians 5:15-17, we can conclude that it has to do with being wise and not foolish. Webster elaborates a bit more on the word "circumspect." It means, "Attentive to all circumstances or consequences; discreet; cautious." Now we have a good picture of how every Christian should walk—but especially the newly singled!

It took a few years of growing up, of maturing, before I mastered the art of being friendly with just a touch of reserve. It is still easy for me to talk to strangers but the puppy dog friendliness has been laid to rest.

Having learned my lesson through the first trauma, I was better prepared to face the aftereffects of the second. I wasn't sure if being divorced rather than widowed would make a difference, but at least I was in control and "attentive to all circumstances." I have had the complete support, understanding and friendship of the people in my church. The men are sincerely friendly—and so are their wives. It is a very comfortable, at-peace-with-myself position to be in.

Your hurt may still be so fresh that you have not been able to analyze your own actions and reactions. Stand back and take a good look at yourself. Then practice being openly and honestly friendly—and with the men, add just a touch of reserve.

How to belong to your church? Face the facts with the pastor and be assured of a warm welcome. Find your place of service within the church. Accept the few restrictions for divorced people with understanding and Christian love. Don't blame the church or the people in it for your misfortune. Rise above it with the Lord's help and earn the respect of your fellow members by walking in love; walking in the light of God's Word—and by walking ever so cautiously in your relationships with the opposite sex.

Don't hold back—go ahead and *belong* to your church!

13

Often Alone,
But Seldom Lonely

"Whither shall I go from thy Spirit? Or whither shall I flee from thy presence? If I ascend up into heaven, thou art there; if I make my bed in sheol, behold, thou art there. If I take the wings of the morning, and dwell in the uttermost parts of the sea, Even there shall thy hand lead me, and thy right hand shall hold me."

Psalms 139:7-10

Alone—at last! Sometimes I walk in the door of my home and the absolute stillness greets me like a dear friend, or a breath of fresh air. If my day at work has been hectic, filled with one meeting after another, with decisions and deadlines to be made and met, I look forward with relish to the evening, when I can be alone.

After you have stopped fighting all of the emotional battles, and find that your recovery is a fact of life, you discover that there are some advantages to living alone. The house is much easier to keep clean and the laundry is only half the work. You can eat when and what you want—or not at all. Any money left after the bills are paid is yours to spend, invest, or give away. You can read a book, or watch television. And the program is yours alone to choose. If you are not careful, you will begin to like it!

I have to admit that I enjoy living alone. My life is full and I am happy. The few evenings, or hours, that I have to myself are delightful. I will never have time to do all of the things I have up my sleeve. Sounds like Utopia, doesn't it? Not quite. There is another side to the coin. Once you have been a part of a pair, and no longer are, you will have times when you are lonely. Lonely for what was, or what might have been.

Before we begin to feel sorry for ourselves, however, let's take a good look at this intangible thing called loneliness. It is not reserved for the formerly married. Nor do you have to be alone to experience it. You can be lonely in marriage as well as out. Some of the loneliest people in the world are surrounded by a crowd. You can even feel it within the family circle. Few people, if any, can say they are never lonely.

Will you agree, then, that being alone is not the same as being lonely? Alone simply means that you are not in the presence of others. Lonely means that you are depressed by this fact. How to be alone and not lonely is something you have to learn. You can't learn it overnight. It takes time and determination. And an awareness of the presence of the Lord Jesus Christ. If I feel a trifle down at being alone I return to the 139th Psalm and read verses 7 through 10.

"Whither shall I go from thy Spirit? Or whither shall I flee from thy presence? If I ascend up into heaven, thou art there; if I make my bed in sheol, behold, thou art there. If I take the wings of the morning, and dwell in the uttermost parts of the sea, Even there shall thy hand lead me, and thy right hand shall hold me." Sometimes I start singing, "No never a-lo-o-one." Then, I get busy!

When you realize that loneliness is no respecter of persons—or marital status—it helps. What makes one person feel lonely, may not affect you at all. I'm sure that if we could switch the pictures of our memory off like we do the television set, it would also help. Then, we each have certain days, or dates, that trigger the reaction of loneliness.

Vi and I were discussing this one day and we agreed that one of the loneliest times is when couple-friends celebrate their anniversaries. It is such a twosome occasion. I miss the

Sweetheart/Birthday cards I used to receive. And for some silly reason our church's Easter breakfast is hard for me to attend. But the days when I feel lonely can be counted on one hand.

Places can have the same effect on people. We, lived in San Francisco for two years during World War II. Bob was in the Navy and was stationed there. We used to walk hand-in-hand through the fog—all three of us. I always feel lonely when I visit that beautiful city.

Ray and I had visited Ronnie and Mary in Costa Rica on two occasions. This year, when I returned alone, I was surprised to experience the feeling that something, or someone, was missing.

Sometimes it is good to face dates, days and places head-on that have a way of making you feel alone and depressed. Visiting with my dear friends, Ralph and Jerry Horn, in San Jose, California, a few years ago, I asked Jerry if she would take me back to the house where Bob and I had lived in San Francisco. We had a little trouble locating it, but when we reached the foot of the hill, I asked her to wait while I climbed to the top. As I walked, I remembered the many times Bob and I had gone up and down that incline together. When I reached the house, I discovered it was for sale. I counted the steps, eighteen in all, as I slowly approached the door. For a few minutes, I relived those happy days when the three Rosses lived high on a hill in San Francisco. I have never been back, but I'm glad I faced that lonely moment.

If I were to spend too much time in the past, I would be often lonely. As it is, I am alone and seldom lonely. Oh, there are times when I wish for male companionship. I wouldn't be honest with you, if I denied it. A candlelight dinner on the top of one of Denver's skyscrapers would be great—with the right man.

There are other times when I miss a husband. But, for the most part, I am a contented single person.

Shortly after I moved into my new condominium, I had an experience that almost sent me to the computerized mating service. The laundryroom was in the process of being papered. When I returned home after work, the dryer was sitting in the middle of the floor and the papering only about half done. Before long, the telephone rang. It was the paper hanger.

"Amy, did you find that mouse?"

I was sitting on the stool at my kitchen counter and my feet automatically moved to the top rung.

"What mouse? " I screeched.

"The one that was under your dryer," he replied.

He assured me that the mouse was dead and even decomposed, but I couldn't bring myself down off of that stool to look. I just took his word for it. Oh, for a nice, brave husband! Since I didn't have one, I put in a panic call to Cliff Norris, manager of the art department at the publishing house. He and his wife live close by. Within minutes he was at my door with a plastic bag. He removed the evidence and washed the floor. Crisis past!

Mice, or loneliness, may provide the motive for remarriage, but learn to be alone and happy before you make that jump. For many newly singled people this takes a bit of doing. You will arrive at this position after you have settled all the doubts you have about yourself and can honestly say, "I like being me." That's what it is all about. If you don't find yourself, and like what you find, you will never be able to enjoy living, or being alone.

14

Finding Myself

"Search me, O God, and know my heart; try me, and know my thoughts; And see if there be any wicked way in me, and lead me in the way everlasting."

Pslams 139:23,24

Children seldom worry about who they are. With a flick of their imagination they can become anyone they please. Young people today often struggle with the question, "Who am I?" When I married Bob—I knew who I was. Mrs. L. Robert Ross. We were as different as night and day. Bob was even-tempered, tender, kindly firm—and fun to live with. I had a temper and I was outgoing, efficient, always heading up something—and fun to live with.

It never occurred to me that I should try to change Bob. I loved him just the way he was. Outside of my temper, he applauded my every effort. And in his quiet, firm way—in one short hour—he taught me how to control that temper. At home, a temper tantrum usually had produced what I wanted—attention. Being a firsthand witness to such a scene before we were married, Bob warned, "Don't try to pull that after we're married."

Shortly after Ronnie was born, I did. The reason—my hair would not do what I wanted it to. I threw the comb on the floor, myself across the bed and bawled. Nothing happened. I stopped and listened. The house was unbelievably quiet. Bob had gone for a walk. End of temper tantrums.

We had spats, but never a "problem." But then, nobody was writing books and articles telling us how to "handle" each other. Women's liberation and male chauvinism were unheard of. We were happily "at home" with each other and our two opposite personalities blended into one complete person.

After Bob was gone I didn't go back to being exactly the same person I was before we were married, nor did I want to. I could only be a better person for having lived with him for those ten years. But without him as my ballast, I had to find my own single self. Youth was on my side and I gradually made the transition from Bob's widow to Amy A. Ross, mother and business woman. Finding myself was not too difficult for I had never lost the real "me" with Bob.

Then Ray came into my life. We had been in the same church as teenagers, but had not seen each other for years. His first question, "Amy, how come you have never remarried?" Half jokingly, I replied, "My friends tell me I am too self-sufficient. I scare men away."

"You don't scare me one bit," he answered with a most charming smile. "Will you have dinner with me tonight?" And, of course, I did.

He was outgoing, efficient, an organizer; he had a temper—and he was fun to go with. He was nothing like Bob and too much like me.

Three years later we were married. It wasn't long before I realized that two such strong personalities cannot survive under the same roof in harmony. One of us was going to have to change. I didn't deliberately set out to change, it was just the path of least resistance. A letter I received from Ray when he was out of town on business acknowledged that change. Here is just a part of that letter.

Your devotion to me, evidenced by the changes you have made in the years we have been married, has spoken loud and clear. No one knows better than I do that it has been you who has given in the most, and given of the most. I only trust that in all of it the love that has grown in my heart has been ample to compensate for that which you have given.

I realize I have peculiarities unlike almost anyone else, but they are a part of me, and a part that even though willing to change, I find I cannot. It has been because you are willing to accept, or put up with them, that our marriage is as it is.

I don't wear any blue ribbons for those changes. I could not have "given in" if I had not had my work at the publishing house as an outlet for the real me. And it wasn't even the wise thing to do. Instead of changing my personality to keep peace, we should have found a way to accept each other as we were and been able to build an honest relationship.

Instead, I no longer headed up things, yet I wanted to. I became the "quiet one" at social gatherings, but it was no fun. I stepped aside to make room for his efficiency and lost my self-confidence. I soon developed five thumbs on each hand. While Bob had always played for fun, I played to win. So did Ray. I soon stopped competing and lost the challenge. The change was gradual, but very real.

Sitting on the floor in Ronnie and Mary's apartment one evening after the separation, Ronnie remarked, "I never could figure out how you could be the efficient woman executive at work and turn into a lamb the minute you walked in the door of your home."

The first week or two after moving into the duplex I began to realize how much I had suppressed the real me. Not only was I going to have to adjust to being alone again, but I had to find my way out of that shell I had crawled into during the past nine years. More than once I found myself looking in the mirror and asking, "Hey, who are you?"

And as the Lord so graciously led me through each step of

recovery, He also answered this question. I am business woman, mother, daughter and friend. I need not feel unloved, rejected, unwanted or incomplete. I am a sinner saved by grace. A child of God. And while God was reassuring me of my identity, He also answered question number two.

"Why again, Lord?"

A two-time loser, once by death and again by divorce. Was I destined to live out the rest of my life alone? Then He began to show me the truth of Romans 8:28.

"And we know that all things work together for good to them that love God, to them who are the called according to his purpose."

Dr. Verrill once told me that the "all things" are the adverse things, the tragedies, the problems of life. Good things don't have to "work together for good." They are already good. But God uses the hurt, the heartache to bring us blessing.

I am one of many ". . . who are the called according to his purpose." God has a plan for my life—a purpose. I may throw a monkey wrench into His plan at times, but He takes my mistakes and turns them around into something good. And as I face the hurt He reminds me that His ". . . grace is sufficient . . ." for me. Then He sets me back on the course He has for my life.

It was fun rediscovering my own self again. As the months passed, life took on new meaning. I was free to follow the Lord's leading. Psalm 116:16 summed it up for me. "O Lord, truly I am thy servant; I am thy servant, . . . thou hast loosed my bonds."

Finding yourself may not be a necessary part of your recovery, but for many newly singled people it is. An unhappy marriage can be ended by death—or divorce. If part of that unhappiness was due to your inability to be yourself with your partner, then you will no doubt need to find the answer to "Who am I?" Ask the Lord to help you and slowly begin to uncover the real you.

The last two verses of Psalm 139 were David's prayer. They can well be ours. "Search me, O God, and know my heart; try me, and know my thoughts; And see if there be any wicked way in me, and lead me in the way everlasting."

God has a way of sanding off the rough edges when we ask Him to. Knowing yourself is not enough. You must end up liking yourself. It's no fun living with someone you don't like, even if it is you.

I asked a friend one day, "Do you like yourself?" His reaction was interesting. He was hesitant to say "Yes" for fear I would misunderstand. He obviously didn't want to say "No" because he might then have to explain why. I laughed and quickly confided, "Well, I like me."

If you are ever going to recover from the hurt of losing your mate, you must enjoy your own company, have respect for yourself and be able to say, "I like me." God made us with this capacity. He also used this self-love to help us understand how we are to love others. It is so important that He stated it as the second great commandment. To keep it in its proper place, however, let's read the first as well.

"And thou shalt love the Lord thy God with all thy heart, and with all thy soul, and with all thy mind, and with all thy strength: this is the first commandment. And the second is this: Thou shalt love thy neighbor as thyself. There is no other commandment greater than these" (Mark 12:30,31).

When you can answer the question "Who am I?" to your own satisfaction and begin to see God's purpose in allowing you to hurt, you can then write "recovered" across your case history. If your loss is recent, don't be discouraged if recovery seems impossible. It will come. Stay close to the Lord and let the healing of His love do the work. He has a plan and a purpose for you.

In a letter analyzing the manuscript for this book, my son wrote:

> One of the hardest parts of being a writer is having something to say. You have to have lived a bit. And that, you know, has nothing to do with years, but rather with the road one travels down. Part of your "living a bit" was the loss of two mates in different ways. That certainly gives you more to say than the average contented housewife. There is something to

be said for tragedy. There is an Arabic saying which reminds us that a life into which no rain falls soon becomes a desert. Your life is certainly no desert.

As a young man I often tried to make some sense out of my father's premature death. How had *I* benefited by it? Would God do that to ME for no reason? Later I was able to ask why God would allow that to happen to US. I have since wondered what you would be today if you had not been forced to make it on your own. Another contented housewife? And, as pleasant as that may sound, what would you then have had to share?

It has occurred to me that we are all made of metal, some good, others mediocre. When God wants to make a tool, He has to temper the metal. There is little reason to temper mediocre metal, because all the tempering in the world won't make it good. But those whose quality is high had better get ready. Because what's comin' ain't no fun at all. They are about to get tempered! And that fire is hot. And after they are hot, He hits them with a hammer. And they only become tools after a lot of hammering. You've been hammered on a lot, and though at times it may seem a dubious honor, being a tool is better than being a chunk of metal. That's just a bit of "practical theology." If I had my choice, and I say this with fear and trembling, I'd rather be heated up and pounded on . . .

I love you,

Ron

Allowing for the bias of my number one and only son, his letter started me thinking. Could the double trauma of my life be God's way of making me the kind of tool He can use for His glory? I pray so.

Would you face your loss, your tragedy, your heartache with this same bit of "practical theology"? And then let's both make

II Thessalonians 1:11 and 12 our prayer.

"Wherefore, also, we pray always for you, that our God would count you worthy of this calling, and fulfill all the good pleasure of his goodness, and the work of faith with power. That the name of our Lord Jesus Christ may be glorified in you, and ye in him, according to the grace of our God and the Lord Jesus Christ."